D0596949

DUKE

DAILY DEVOTIONS FOR DIE-HARD FANS

BLUE DEVILS

DUKE

To the Revs. Scott and
Mary Jane Wilson-Parsons,
who came along and changed everything

Daily Devotions for Die-Hard Fans: Duke Blue Devils
© 2010, 2014 Ed McMinn
Extra Point Publishers; P.O. Box 871; Perry GA 31069

Cover design by John Powell and Slynn McMinn
Interior design by Slynn McMinn

Visit us at www.die-hardfans.com.

BLUE DEVILS

Daily Devotions for Die-Hard Fans

ACC
Clemson Tigers
Duke Blue Devils
FSU Seminoles
Georgia Tech Yellow Jackets
North Carolina Tar Heels
NC State Wolfpack
Virginia Cavaliers
Virginia Tech Hokies

BIG 10
Michigan Wolverines
Ohio State Buckeyes

BIG 12
Baylor Bears
Oklahoma Sooners
Oklahoma State Cowboys
TCU Horned Frogs
Texas Longhorns
Texas Tech Red Raiders

SEC
Alabama Crimson Tide
Arkansas Razorbacks
Auburn Tigers
More Auburn Tigers
Florida Gators
Georgia Bulldogs
More Georgia Bulldogs
Kentucky Wildcats
LSU Tigers
Mississippi State Bulldogs
Missouri Tigers
Ole Miss Rebels
South Carolina Gamecocks
More South Carolina Gamecocks
Texas A&M Aggies
Tennessee Volunteers

NASCAR

DUKE

DAILY DEVOTIONS FOR DIE-HARD FANS

BLUE DEVILS

IN THE BEGINNING

Read Genesis 1, 2:1-3.

"God saw all that he had made, and it was very good" (v. 1:31).

Football, track and field, gymnastics, bowling, swimming, fencing, and volleyball — Wilbur Wade "Cap" Card introduced them all to Trinity University. In 1905, he added one more sport to the list: basketball.

Card arrived at Trinity in 1895 and while he was an undergraduate, he participated in baseball and track. Along the way, he decided to forego a career as a Methodist minister and instead make athletics his life's profession.

In 1905, the basketball coach at Wake Forest suggested to Card that the two teams play a game. Trinity had no basketball team, so Card simply organized one. The game was so new that in an article about the sports, the school newspaper, the *Chronicle*, felt it wise to inform the students that "unlike baseball, the game is played most often at night."

The school gymnasium underwent a few changes to accommodate the new sport, which the *Chronicle* described as "one of the most fascinating and intensely interesting indoor sports known today." Iron guards were fastened around the gym's lights, and detachable goals were constructed and attached.

A photograph of Card's first team showed eight players, none of whom had ever played basketball before. Card was hampered somewhat in organizing his team because some of the school's best athletes were involved with baseball. The Trinity players practiced three weeks for their inaugural game, which was played at Trinity's Angier Duke Gym, built in 1898 and today known as The Ark. Only about one-third the size of today's courts, the floor was so small it was possible to shoot from one end to the other.

Wake Forest won 24-10, but one of college sport's greatest traditions -- Duke basketball -- had begun.

Beginnings are important, but what we make of them is even more important. Consider, for example, how far the Duke basketball program has come since that first game. Every morning, you get a gift from God: a new beginning. God hands to you as an expression of divine love a new day full of promise and the chance to right the wrongs in your life. You can use the day to pay a debt, start a new relationship, replace a burned-out light bulb, tell your family you love them, chase a dream, solve a nagging problem . . . or not.

God simply provides the gift. How you use it is up to you. People often talk wistfully and quite sincerely about starting over or making a new beginning. God gives you the chance to do just that with the dawning of every new day. You have the chance today to make right a lot of things in your life – and that includes your relationship with God.

It is well-nigh a certainty that Trinity is to have another game added to her list of athletic sports in the near future. The game is basketball.
— *The* Chronicle *on Jan. 30, 1906*

Every day is not just a dawn; it is a precious chance to start over or begin anew.

NECESSARY THINGS

Read Luke 18:18-29.

"You still lack one thing. Sell everything you have and give to the poor, and you will have treasure in heaven. Then come, follow me" (v. 22).

Hired to be Duke's new head basketball coach, Mike Krzyzewski called his wife, Mickie, to give her the exciting news. She went right to the heart of the interview/hiring process and learned that one absolutely necessary component of the job had not been discussed or decided upon: the new coach's salary.

When Bill Foster resigned as Duke's head coach at the end of the 1980 season, Duke Athletic Director Tom Butters asked Indiana's Bobby Knight if he would be interested in the job. Knight declined, but he recommended a 32-year-old coach who had played for him at Army, had been on his staff at IU, and was now the head coach at West Point: Mike Krzyzewski.

Reluctant to commit to a coach coming off a 9-17 season against competition that wasn't of ACC caliber, Butters interviewed Krzyzewski three times. Shortly after the coach left his office the third time, Butters told Steve Vacendak, who was about to become the associate athletic director, to go to the airport and get Krzyzewski. "You're not going to interview him again?" an incredulous Vacendak asked. "No, I'm going to hire him," Butters replied.

"Will you accept this job?" Butters asked a rather bewildered Krzyzewski when he returned. The coach immediately said yes, leading Butters to protest, "Wait a minute; we haven't talked about salary." Krzyzewski said, "You'll be fair."

Thus, when the man who would be Coach K called his wife and she asked about his salary, he could only reply honestly, "I don't know. We didn't discuss it."

It's possible in a job interview to omit discussion of some quite necessary things since there are usually so many factors to consider. It's that way in other areas of our lives too.

Like the ruler who approached Jesus, we clutter our lives with things, with trinkets, with toys; we surround ourselves with stuff. We take up the days of our lives with quite legitimate work: making a living, paying the bills, maintaining a home, taking care of the kids, planning for the future. But in staying so busy we often allow ourselves to omit from our lives what is truly necessary and precious.

Nothing is more necessary or more important in our lives than God and our relationship with him. Thus, the necessary things in our life include learning God's truth and growing as a Christian, loving not just our family members but those around us and reaching out to them with the truth of Jesus' salvation, and obeying God's word in our lives.

No matter how full it may seem, a life without God and Jesus is empty.

From what we get, we can make a living; what we give, however, makes a life.
— *Arthur Ashe*

**Material wealth, possessions, and busy schedules
can clutter a life, but they can never fill it.**

YOU NEVER KNOW

Read Exodus 3:1-12.

"But Moses said to God, 'Who am I, that I should go to Pharaoh and bring the Israelites out of Egypt?' And God said, 'I will be with you'" (vv. 11-12a).

Any hopes Patrick Bailey may have had about a pro football career surely went down with his knee against Wake Forest his senior season. But then, you never know.

Bailey was a four-year letterman for the Blue Devils and a three-year starter at defensive end. He was a hard worker who practiced so diligently during preseason two-a-days that he would lose five to ten pounds per practice.

Bailey was an Academic All-ACC Player who had two reasons for leaving Texas to come east: "The football team plus academics brought me here." As a junior in 2006, he was Duke's co-Most Outstanding Defensive Player, finishing third on the team in tackles and leading the team in sacks and quarterback pressures.

While he was at Duke, Bailey was active in Athletes in Action. "Shoot," he said, letting one of his Texas expressions creep into his speech, "religion is a big part of my life."

Bailey needed both his religion and his propensity for hard work to keep him going after the Wake Forest game of Saturday, Oct. 6., 2007. He was off to a great start his senior season. After five games, he was in the top ten in the ACC in both sacks and tackles for loss. Against Wake, though, he suffered a knee injury that ended his season and probably ended his football career. Especially when he went undrafted.

But with Patrick Bailey, you never know. He didn't give up, rehabbed his knee, and signed a free-agent contract with the Pittsburgh Steelers. Not only did he make the roster, he was the team's Rookie of the Year in 2008.

You never know what you can do until – like Patrick Bailey – you want to bad enough or until – like Moses -- you have to. Serving in the military, maybe even in combat. Standing by a friend while everyone else unjustly excoriates her. Making a pro football team after being overlooked. Undergoing agonizing medical treatment and managing to smile. You never know what life will demand of you.

It's that way too in your relationship with God. As Moses discovered, you never know where or when God will call you or what God will ask of you. You do know that God expects you to be faithful and willing to trust him even when he calls you to tasks that daunt and dismay you.

No matter what, though, you can respond faithfully to whatever God calls you to do for him. That's because even though you never know what lies ahead, you do know that God will lead you and provide you what you need -- and bless you along the way.

I wanted to get that shot and this is my opportunity, so I have to go out there and make the best of what chance I have.
— Patrick Bailey on signing a free-agent contract with the Steelers

**You never know what God will ask you to do,
but you always know he will provide
everything you need to do it.**

THE BAD GUYS

Read Ephesians 6:10-18.

"Our struggle is not against flesh and blood, but against the rulers, against the authorities, against the powers of this dark world and against the spiritual forces of evil in the heavenly realms" (v. 12).

If you're among the chosen few who are fortunate enough to play men's basketball for Duke, then you better understand that when you put on that jersey, you become a bad guy.

It's just a fact of Duke basketball life. In a survey on Match.com in 2010, five percent of singles looking for a relationship said cheering for Duke would kill the deal. In 2010, detestation of all things Blue Devil reached its zenith prior to the Final Four. The week of the games columnists and bloggers repeatedly came up with reasons for folks across the country to pull against Duke. One columnist compared Mike Krzyzewski to the devil.

"Once again, Duke [was] being cast as the team to hate."

But the hostility to all things Duke in 2010 was neither something new or at a level equal to that of the past. "These guys don't have it quite as bad as we used to," declared assistant coach Chris Collins, a guard from 1993-96. No fans at the Final Four in Indianapolis in 2010 pelted the Devils with cups and pompoms as they did Christian Laettner and Bobby Hurley in 1992 in Minneapolis. In 2004, Coach K worried that "anti-Duke sentiment had reached a point where it might influence games."

BLUE DEVILS

Why would Duke be so consistently vilified? Duh. They win. Duke is among the few basketball programs in the country that is the favorite virtually every time it walks onto a court. "Underdog" and "Duke basketball" just don't go together. Bad guys or not, the 2010 Duke team made sure the antipathy would continue in the best possible way: They won Duke's fourth national title.

While fans and writers may cast Duke as basketball's bad guys, they speak in terms of having fun by pulling against the favorite, not in the sense of true evil. Evil does exist, which obviously means its existence is tolerated by a just and good God. Why this is so remains one of the great conundrums of our faith.

Evil is not intrinsically a part of God's physical world, which God declared to be "good." Rather, evil is a function of the spirit world, of Satan and his minions. Human beings are thus the pawns in an ongoing cosmic struggle between good and evil. The primary battleground is our hearts. This is why we struggle with evil even after we surrender our lives to Christ. The forces of evil don't concede defeat; they work harder.

The day of God's own choosing will come when all evil will be defeated and goodness will rule unopposed. Not only will the spiritual forces of evil be eradicated, but so will those humans who have aligned themselves with them. Evil is for losers.

If we're going to be despised or hated by anybody because we go to school and we want to win, you know what? That's your problem.
— Mike Krzyzewski

Evil may win temporarily — even in your heart —
but to follow Jesus is to live daily
in the knowledge of good's ultimate triumph.

THE GREATEST

Read Mark 9:33-37.

"If anyone wants to be first, he must be the very last, and the servant of all" (v. 35).

Duke-Kentucky was the greatest college game of them all." As the years have passed, little has happened that would challenge that sportswriter's assessment.

He was speaking of the matchup in the finals of the NCAA's 1992 East Regional Finals. It isn't just the unbelievable ending that bolsters the game's claim to being the greatest college game ever; play throughout the game – not just at the end – was exceptional. Duke shot 65 percent from the field; Kentucky shot 57 percent. Christian Laettner was a perfect 10 for 10 from the floor and 10 of 10 from the line for 31 points.

With 19.6 seconds left in overtime, Kentucky pulled off a three-point play to lead 101-100. Laettner then made two free throws with 7.8 seconds left. Many must have thought those were the game winners. Not even close. Kentucky guard Sean Woods banked a hook shot in for a 103-02 lead. As it turned out, his only mistake was that he gave Duke too much time: 2.1 seconds.

As his players gathered for a time out, Coach Mike Krzyzewski told them, "We're going to win this game, and here's how we're going to do it." He called for what has become known in Duke lore as "THE Play."

It consisted simply of a 70-foot pass from Grant Hill to Laettner at the foul line. He would turn and shoot. The play had been tried against Wake Forest and had failed. What was different this time, however, was that Kentucky chose not to guard Hill; he could see his target clearly. Hill fired a strike. Laettner had time to dribble to his left before he spun and nailed the 18-foot jumper that became "the most famous shot in collegiate history."

After winning the greatest game ever, Duke was on its way to the Final Four and eventually another national championship.

We all want to be the greatest. The goal for the Blue Devils and their fans every season is the national championship. The competition at work is to be the most productive sales person on the staff or the Teacher of the Year. In other words, we define being the greatest in terms of the struggle for personal success. It's nothing new; the disciples saw greatness in the same way.

As Jesus illustrated, though, greatness in the Kingdom of God has nothing to do with the world's understanding of success. Rather, the greatest are those who channel their ambition toward the furtherance of Christ's kingdom through love and service, rather than their own advancement, which is a complete reversal of status and values as the world sees them.

After all, who could be greater than the person who has Jesus for a brother and God for a father? And that's every one of us.

No other college game has ever combined, in one package, this much meaning, this much expertise and this much drama.
— Columnist Bob Ryan on the 1992 Duke-UK game

**To be great for God has nothing to do
with personal advancement and everything to do
with the advancement of Christ's kingdom.**

THE PRIZE

Read Philippians 3:10-16.

"I press on toward the goal to win the prize for which God has called me heavenward in Christ Jesus" (v. 14).

Every time she walked into Cameron Indoor Stadium and looked up, Lindsey Harding was inspired by what she saw. Now she hopes others are similarly inspired by the same prize that has been accorded to her.

What Harding saw hanging inside the stadium was Alana Beard's retired jersey, No. 20. Beard is a Duke basketball legend. She was the National Player of the Year as a senior in 2004; she was All-America three times and the ACC Female Athlete of the Year in both 2003 and 2004. She set a school scoring record of 2,687 points. Beard was the first player in NCAA basketball history with more than 2,600 points, 500 assists, and 400 steals. Her four years at Duke were among the school's greatest as they won four ACC titles and reached the Final Four twice.

Harding saw that retired No. 20 jersey innumerable times in her career at Duke. It spoke to her of confidence: "Look what she did and the impact she had. Maybe I can do it."

She did. On Jan. 20, 2008, at halftime of the N.C. State game, Harding's No. 10 was formally retired and hoisted to the Cameron rafters. As a senior in 2007, Harding was both the National Player of the Year and the National Defensive Player of the Year. She set a new school record with 579 assists. She was the point guard on the legendary 2006-07 team that went undefeated in the regular season. Michigan State women's basketball coach Joanne P. Mc-Callie said Harding "had the best senior season I've ever seen of any player in the history of women's basketball."

Now Harding hopes the honor of having her jersey retired and the sight of it hanging in Cameron does for others what Beard's did for her: inspire them to Duke basketball greatness.

Even the most modest and self-effacing among us can't help but be pleased by prizes and honors. They symbolize the approval and appreciation of others, whether it's a retired jersey, an Employee of the Month trophy, a plaque for sales achievement, or the sign declaring yours as the neighborhood's prettiest yard.

Such prizes and awards are often the culmination of the pursuit of personal achievement and accomplishment. They represent accolades and recognition from the world. Nothing is inherently wrong with any of that as long as we keep them in perspective.

That is, we must never let awards become such idols that we worship or lower our sight from the greatest prize of all and the only one truly worth winning. It's one that won't rust, collect dust, or leave us wondering why we worked so hard to win it in the first place. The ultimate prize is eternal life, and it's ours through Jesus Christ.

It's overwhelming. I'm going to be really happy and overjoyed to see that my name is going to be there forever.
— *Lindsey Harding on learning her No. 10 would be retired*

The greatest prize of all doesn't require competition to claim it; God has it ready to hand to you through Jesus Christ.

EXCUSES, EXCUSES

Read Luke 9:57-62.

"Another said, 'I will follow you, Lord; but first let me go back and say good-by to my family'" (v. 61).

The Blue Devils once had a rather novel excuse for losing to North Carolina: They blamed the Tar Heel student manager.

The game of Feb. 9, 1957, was a landmark in the rivalry. UNC Comptroller Billy Carmichael, Jr., and Bill Friday, president of the state's Consolidated University System, believed that college basketball could be a success on TV. To prove it, they decided to broadcast the Duke-UNC game over local public TV, the first basketball game of any kind on television. The process was called "Broadvision"; it had no audio but fans could watch while listening to the play-by-play on the radio.

To pull it off, the two men used "hammers and picks to chisel a hole in the cinderblock wall behind the bleachers in Woollen Gym so they could fit the lens of the Broadvision camera." Viewers in Raleigh, Greensboro, and Charlotte were thus able to tune in and watch a black-and-white telecast with a camera lens that never moved.

The game was a great one with a strange ending. Duke rallied from an eight-point deficit in the last two minutes with guard Bobby Joe Harris turning two steals into baskets to tie the game at 73. After his last basket, Harris rushed back on defense and glanced over to the hand-operated wooden scoreboard beside the

Carolina bench. It read "UNC 73, Duke 71."

Harris thus believed the Devils were two points behind with only seconds to play, so he made the logical move: He committed a foul. Carolina made both free throws for the 75-73 win. The UNC student manager had simply gotten so caught up in the game he had failed to flip the score over after Harris' last basket.

A frustrated Harris admitted he wouldn't have committed the foul if he had realized the score was tied.

Has some of your most creative thinking sometimes involved inventing excuses for not going in to work? Have you discovered that an unintended benefit of computers is that you can always blame them for the destruction of all your hard work? Don't you manage to stammer or stutter some justification when a state trooper pulls you over? We're usually pretty good at making excuses to cover our failures or to get out of something we don't particularly want to do.

That holds true for our faith life also. The Bible is too hard to understand so I won't read it; the weather's too pretty to be shut up in church; praying in public is embarrassing and I'm not very good at it anyway.

The plain truth is, though, that whatever excuses we make for not following Jesus wholeheartedly are not good enough. That's because Jesus made no excuses to avoid dying for us; we should thus as his followers offer none to avoid living for him.

UNC didn't beat us. Their scorekeeper did.
— *Bobby Joe Harris*

**Try though we might, no excuses can justify
our failure to follow Jesus wholeheartedly.**

ONE TOUGH COOKIE

Read 2 Corinthians 11:21b-29.

"Besides everything else, I face daily the pressure of my concern for all the churches" (v. 28).

Nate James "brought a warrior mentality to the court." No wonder. He learned his toughness from a Marine.

James played in 135 games from 1997-2001, starting 63 of them. He was a two-time captain; as a senior in the national championship season of 2000-01, he was All-ACC and a member of the ACC All-Defensive Team.

That latter award was no surprise considering the "leatherneck attitude" James brought to the court. After all, he went to boot camp in his back yard.

James' father was a 212-pound Marine master sergeant who could bench press 365 pounds. His son was a skinny 13-year-old when the two went at each other one on one. "He had this 'I'm gonna dunk on you' idea," Sr. said. "I'd say it would never happen, give him a foul, and bounce him off the court a little." That is, dad never took it easy on his overmatched son. But he also had a purpose in the competition and the aggression. "I gave him a sample of what it would be like [physically] at a different level," said Sr.

That was the Marine-tough mentality James brought to Duke, but he also arrived equipped with the team approach of the Corps. Late in James' senior year, Coach Mike Krzyzewski benched him in favor of a freshman to make the lineup quicker. James not only accepted the move but went to the freshman and offered his support. "When I heard about that, I almost cried," Krzyzewski said. "Where do you find a kid like that?"

James joined the Blue Devils' coaching staff in May 2008. One of the attributes Krzyzewski said James brought to the program was his toughness.

You don't have to be a great Duke basketball player like Nate James to be tough. In America today, toughness isn't restricted to physical accomplishments and brute strength. Going to work every morning even when you feel bad, sticking by your rules for your children in a society that ridicules parental authority, making hard decisions about your aging parents' care — you've got to be tough every day just to live honorably, decently, and justly.

Living faithfully requires toughness, too, though in America chances are you won't be imprisoned, stoned, or flogged this week for your faith as Paul was. Still, contemporary society exerts subtle, psychological, daily pressures on you to turn your back on your faith and your values. Popular culture promotes promiscuity, atheism, and gutter language; your children's schools have kicked God out; the corporate culture advocates amorality before the shrine of the almighty dollar.

You have to hang tough to keep the faith.

Ask him to run through a wall and he would do it.
— Duke assistant coach Steve Wojciechowski on Nate James the player

Life demands more than mere physical toughness;
you must be spiritually tough too.

HEAVENBOUND

Read Revelation 21:1-7.

"Then I saw a new heaven and a new earth, for the first heaven and the first earth had passed away" (v. 1).

Gene Banks had such a great Senior Night that he said it was close to Heaven.

Banks is the only player in Duke men's basketball history to be on the school's career top ten lists for points, rebounds, assists, and steals. He was the ACC Rookie of the Year in 1978, and during the magical run to the Final Four that season, he became the first active Duke athlete to appear on the cover of *Sports Illustrated*. He was All-ACC and All-America as a senior in 1981. In 1994, he was inducted into the Duke Sports Hall of Fame.

Before the game on Senior Night Feb. 28, 1981, Banks prayed, "God, give me the opportunity to leave these people with a good memory." God certainly answered that prayer. The memories started before the game. Banks had often thrown roses to the crowd in high school, so he took a rose to each Cameron corner, further spiking an already sky-high crowd.

Mike Krzyzewski's first team was only 14-11; the opponent was 11th-ranked UNC. In the last half, Carolina took a nine-point lead and appeared to be on the way to a win. "That's when it kicked in to me that I was going to die out there," Banks said. "They were going to have to carry me out before we would lose this game."

The Blue Devils clawed back but still trailed by two with only one second left. After a time out, Kenny Dennard hit Banks with a perfect pass; Banks buried a 20-foot jumper at the buzzer. In the overtime, Banks scored six points, including the final two, in the 66-65 win. He finished with 25 points, and the frenzied students carried Banks around Cameron on their shoulders. "This is the closest I've ever been to heaven," he said after the game.

All too often Christians make the mistake of regarding Heaven as an abstract concept simply because they can't really imagine what's it like. Kind of like trying to figure out what God looks like or what Jesus' voice sounds like. But Heaven is a real place, as substantive as that recliner you watch the Blue Devils from or that lawn mower you use to cut the grass.

Certainly we are frustrated that the Bible doesn't contain more information about the believer's ultimate destination. It would be nice to know, for instance, what we'll look like there. But God's Word is much more interested in teaching us how to get to Heaven than in describing exactly what we'll find there. We can know, though, that it's a better place than the one we occupy now.

So why can't we have Heaven on Earth? Here, man's will clashes with God's; the result more often than not is chaos, confusion, and tears. In Heaven, though, God's will is done absolutely. The result is Paradise.

Heaven is real. You better believe it.

When you play a sport, you have two things in mind. One is to get into the Hall of Fame and the other is to go to heaven when you die.
— *Golfer Lee Trevino*

Heaven is a real place where — unlike here on Earth — God's will is done.

NOT WHAT THEY SEEM

Read Habakkuk 1:2-11.

*"Why do you make me look at injustice? Why do you
tolerate wrong? Destruction and violence are before me;
there is strife, and conflict abounds" (v. 3).*

One of the most memorable wins in Duke football history was
helped along by a play that probably wasn't what it seemed.

The Blue Devils of '54 went 7-2-1, buried Nebraska in the Orange
Bowl, and finished the season ranked 14th in the nation. They
were ranked sixth after opening the season by burying Pennsylvania 52-0 and edging Tennessee 7-6. Halfback Bob Pascal, who
was first-team All-ACC, scored the lone Duke touchdown on a
10-yard run. Reserve lineman Jim Nelson kicked the extra point.

But then came a 13-13 tie with fifth-ranked Purdue and a 28-14
loss to 18th-ranked Army. The Blue Devils rallied to whip NC
State 21-7 before they hosted Georgia Tech, which led 20-0 in the
third quarter. Duke coach Bill Murray kept telling his desperate
team to stay intense and breaks would come their way.

First-team All-ACC quarterback Jerry Barger got Duke on the
board with a 12-yard toss to Jerry Kocourek. Then came one of
those breaks Murray had talked about. Tech fumbled, and Duke
recovered at the 35. But the Devils couldn't move, and Barger
dropped back to punt. He was roughed on the kick, which gave
Duke a first down. Or was he? After the game, Barger said, "My
friends said I should have gotten an Oscar for that one. I made

sure the officials knew I had been hit."

Whether the refs saw something that really wasn't there didn't matter. The call stood, Bryant Aldridge scored, and Duke trailed 20-14 with 12:15 left. Duke held and then marched 82 yards. Ed Post scored on a sweep from the four with 50 seconds left. When Nelson converted the extra point, Duke had a 21-20 win, aided in large part by a play that may not have happened at all.

Sometimes in football things just aren't what they seem.

It's that way in life too. In our violent and convulsive times, we must confront the possibility of a new reality: that we are helpless in the face of anarchy; that injustice, destruction, and violence are pandemic in and symptomatic of our modern age. It seems that anarchy is winning, that the system of standards, values, and institutions we have cherished is crumbling while we all we can do is stand around and watch with broken hearts.

But we should not be deceived or disheartened. God is in fact the arch-enemy of chaos, the creator of order and goodness and the architect of all of history. God is in control. We often misinterpret history as the record of mankind's accomplishments – which it isn't – rather than the unfolding of God's plan – which it is. That plan has a clearly defined end: God will make everything right. In that day things will be what they seem.

Unlike any other business in the United States, sports must preserve an illusion of perfect innocence.
— Author Lewis H. Lapham

The forces of good and decency often seem
helpless before evil's power, but don't be fooled:
God is in control and will set things right.

WORK ETHIC

Read Matthew 9:35-38.

"Then he said to his disciples, 'The harvest is plentiful but the workers are few. Ask the Lord of the harvest, therefore, to send out workers into his harvest field'" (vv. 37-38).

Duke head basketball coach Gerry Gerard missed the opening game of the 1948-49 season. He was working another job.

When head football coach Wallace Wade went off to the military in 1942, Eddie Cameron moved in, giving up his position as head basketball coach. Gerard, Cameron's assistant, then moved into the spot his boss vacated.

Gerard had come to Duke in 1931 to run the intramural athletic program. In 1935, he became the coach of the school's first soccer team, leading them for eleven seasons. Gerard coached the basketball team for eight years with an overall record of 131-78. He won two Southern Conference titles in the 19-team league and finished second four other times.

Basketball during World War II was just a little bit different. For instance, when the Blue Devils hosted Wake Forest on a Monday night, only about one hundred folks turned out. A local paper attributed the size of the crowd to its being "fraternity meeting night and no-co-ed night, the feminine students being combined to quarters." Wartime gas rationing also limited the turnout.

Thanks to the Depression, coaches' salaries were also different. Nobody, however, could accuse of Gerard of not working hard to make ends meet. In addition to his soccer and basketball coaching duties, he was a teacher in the school's PE department throughout his career. He also worked as a football, basketball, and track and field official. He did some basketball play-by-play as a radio announcer and managed a Virginia Beach resort in the summer.

Duke opened the 1948-49 season against a team sponsored by Hanes Hosiery, but Gerard missed the game and the practices leading up to it because he was away officiating two football games. His bosses understood the situation and approved his absence. The media had no problem with it either.

Do you embrace hard work or try to avoid it? No matter how hard you may try, you really can't escape hard work. Funny thing about all these labor-saving devices like cell phones and laptop computers: You're working longer and harder than ever. For many of us, our work defines us perhaps more than any other aspect of our lives. But there's a workforce you're a part of that doesn't show up in any Labor Department statistics or any IRS records.

You're part of God's staff; God has a specific job that only you can do for him. It's often referred to as a "calling," but it amounts to your serving God where there is a need in the way that best suits your God-given abilities and talents.

You should stand ready to work for God all the time, 24-7. Those are awful hours, but the benefits are out of this world.

The highest compliment you can pay me is to say I work hard every day.
— *Wayne Gretzky*

God calls you to work for him using the talents and gifts he gave you; whether you're a worker or a malingerer is up to you.

TOLD YOU SO

Read Matthew 24:15-31.

"See, I have told you ahead of time" (v. 25).

Coach Mike Krzyzewski's mom once had the extreme satisfaction of telling her son, "I told you so." He didn't mind one bit.

The Blue Devils of 1990 advanced to the national championship game where they were destroyed by UNLV 103-73. Point guard Bobby Hurley was so distressed by the game that for months afterwards he had nightmares of being chased by sharks.

At that point, Krzyzewski had taken a team to the national title game and had lost both times. After the defeat by UNLV, Emily Krzyzewski sought to console her son by telling him, "That's all right, Son, you'll do better next year." A rather stunned and perhaps somewhat flummoxed Coach K replied, "But Mom, we just played for the national championship."

The season had been a remarkable one, but the Blue Devils had only one way to make their 1990-91 season any better. That was to win it all. They rolled to a 30-7 record but waiting for them in the semifinals were those same Runnin' Rebs from UNLV. They were unbeaten, ranked No. 1, and "widely hailed as the best team since the UCLA juggernauts of the 1960s. No one gave Duke much of a chance."

But "Coach K was so positive, so sure that he convinced us," said Greg Koubek. "By game time we weren't afraid of anything or anybody." Christian Laettner's free throws with 12.7 seconds left were the difference in Duke's 79-77 upset that propelled the Blue Devils into the finals where they met the Kansas Jayhawks. They never trailed and won 72-65.

A laughing, smiling Emily Krzyzewski couldn't wait to rub it in. She told her son, "See, Mike, I told you that you'd do better this time."

Except in cases like Coach K and his mother, don't you just hate it when somebody says, "I told you so"? That means the other person was right and you were wrong; that other person has spoken the truth. You could have listened to that know-it-all in the first place, but then you would have lost the chance yourself to crow, "I told you so," if you were the one who turned out to have spoken the truth.

In our pluralistic age and society, many view truth as relative, meaning absolute truth does not exist. All belief systems have equal value and merit. But this is a ghastly, dangerous fallacy because it ignores the truth that God proclaimed in the presence and words of Jesus.

In speaking the truth, Jesus told everybody exactly what he was going to do: come back and take his faithful followers with him. Those who don't listen or who don't believe will be left behind with those four awful words, "I told you so," ringing in their ears and wringing their souls.

There's nothing in this world more instinctively abhorrent to me than finding myself in agreement with my fellow humans.
— Lou Holtz

Jesus matter-of-factly told us what he has planned:
He will return to gather all the faithful to himself.

DANCING MACHINE

Read 2 Samuel 6:12-22.

"David danced before the Lord with all his might, while he and the entire house of Israel brought up the ark of the Lord with shouts and the sound of trumpets" (vv. 14-15).

Coach Mike Krzyzewski promised his players he'd dance — with a condition. When the season ended, he was true to his word, even if it meant he had to put on his boogie shoes.

The Blue Devils of 2000-01 defeated Southern Cal 79-69 in Philadelphia for a berth in the Final Four. When the team boarded the bus for the ride to the airport, the driver cranked up the Bee Gees' "Staying Alive," which Coach K called "a theme song of sorts" for the team during their NCAA Tournament run. The guys immediately started yelling, "Dance, Coach! Come on, dance!"

But Krzyzewski recalled that two years before, he had "done a little dance" on the bus after the team won the East Regional. They lost in the national championship game. He refused to dance but then relented somewhat. "I'll tell you what," he said. "I'll dance when we win the national championship."

So it was on to Minneapolis where the Blue Devils did indeed win the national title. They rallied for a 95-84 win over Maryland and then rode a 21-point performance from game MVP Mike Dunleavy to an 82-72 defeat of Arizona in the finals.

After the post-game interviews and press commitments, Coach K finally made it to the team bus where his national champions awaited. The guys immediately started to yell: "Come on, Coach. Dance. . . . You promised us." Krzyzewski handed his jacket to his daughter, Jamie, just as "Stayin' Alive" blasted through the bus. "Watch carefully, Jamie," he said. "It's all in the rear end."

And, "as everybody hooted and hollered," Krzyzewski "kept [his] promise and did [his] John Travolta strut down the aisle."

One of the more enduring stereotypes of the Christian is of a dour, sour-faced person always on the prowl to sniff out fun and frivolity and shut it down. "Somewhere, sometime, somebody's having fun — and it's got to stop!" Many understand this to be the mandate that governs the Christian life.

But nothing could be further from reality. Ages ago King David, he who would eventually number Jesus Christ among his house and lineage, set the standard for those who love and worship the Lord when he danced in the presence of God with unrestrained joy.

Many centuries and one savior later, David's example today reminds us that a life spent in an awareness of God's presence is all about celebrating, rejoicing, and enjoying God's countless gifts, including salvation in Jesus Christ.

Yes, dancing can be vulgar and coarse, but as with David, God looks into our hearts to see what is there. Our very life should be one long song and dance for Jesus.

Dancers are the athletes of God.

— *Albert Einstein*

**While dancing and music can be vulgar
and obscene, they can also be inspiring
expressions of abiding love for God.**

THE CHALLENGE

Read Matthew 4:12-25.

"Come, follow me," Jesus said (v. 19).

Duke head coach David Cutcliffe didn't dance around. He came right out and called the North Carolina game his team's biggest challenge of all.

On Nov. 30, 2013, the Blue Devils met the Tar Heels in the program's biggest football game in decades. Ranked 24th, Duke went into the game at 9-2, which tied the school record for wins in a season. A win meant the championship of the ACC's Coastal Division and a berth in the league's title game for the first time. A loss would keep Duke out of the ACC's showcase game. Even without all that pressure, the 6-5 Heels were challenge enough.

"As a competitor," Cutcliffe said before the game, "you want to challenge yourself and see if you're up to the task." The Blue Devils were.

DeVon Edwards returned a kickoff 99 yards for a touchdown that propelled Duke into a 17-15 halftime lead. The margin went to nine in the third quarter when junior wide receiver Jamison Crowder caught his second touchdown pass of the game from quarterback Anthony Boone, this one from 7 yards out.

But the Tar Heels rallied to take a 25-24 lead on a 37-yard field goal with 7:03 to play. Up to the challenge, Duke responded with a 27-yard field goal from Ross Martin that made it 27-25. The Blue Devils then answered one last challenge from UNC when

Edwards pulled down an interception.

Boone took a knee and ran out the clock, and the celebration began with defensive linemen Sydney Sarmiento and Justin Foxx hoisting a Gatorade-soaked Cutcliffe onto their shoulders.

"It's easy to look forward to next week," said left guard Dave Harding, "but right now I think it's OK to kind of revel in what we've just done." What they had done was meet the challenge.

Like the Blue Devil athletic teams every time they take the field or the court, we are challenged daily. Life is a testing ground; God intentionally set it up that way. If we are to grow in character, confidence, and perseverance, and if we are to make a difference in the world, we must meet challenges head-on. Few things in life are as boring and as destructive to our sense of self-worth as a job that doesn't offer any challenges.

Our faith life is the same way. The moment we answered Jesus' call to "Come, follow me," we took on the most difficult challenge we will ever face. We are called to be holy by walking in Jesus' footsteps in a world that seeks to render our Lord irrelevant and his influence negligible. The challenge Jesus places before us is to put our faith and our trust in him and not in ourselves or the transitory values of the secular world.

Daily walking in Jesus' footsteps is a challenge, but the path takes us all the way right up to the gates of Heaven — and then right on through.

No question, this is our greatest challenge.
— David Cutcliffe on the 2013 UNC game

To accept Jesus as Lord is to joyfully take on the challenge of living a holy life in an unholy world.

DAY 15

CLOCKWORK

Read Matthew 25:1-13.

"Keep watch, because you do not know the day or the hour" (v. 13).

Before the age of the shot clock, the Blue Devils occasionally encountered teams that employed the strategy of holding the ball. No one ever pulled off a stall to match what North Carolina State did in 1968.

Both Wake Forest and South Carolina had in the past frozen the ball against Duke. Perhaps most famously (or infamously), in the 1966 ACC semifinals, Dean Smith unveiled his four-corners offense (read "stall") against the top-seeded Blue Devils. (Duke won 21-20 when sophomore center Mike Lewis hit a free throw with four seconds left.)

The Blue Devils of 1968 finished tenth in the nation at 22-6 and second in the league with an 11-3 record. In the first round of the tournament, Clemson slowed the game down before losing 43-40. "Compared with what was to occur against [N.C.] State in the semifinals, [the Clemson game] was a shootout."

The Wolfpack simply held the ball and held it and held it some more. Duke led 4-2 at halftime. As the last half proceeded without a timeout, the radio network simply broke away to run its commercials. "You haven't missed a thing," the play-by-play man said when the break ended.

At one stretch the clocked ticked down fourteen minutes without a shot. The State coach once called a player over to the sideline for some advice. Duke guard Tony Barone followed the player over to his coach and unabashedly listened in on the conversation. The coach didn't seem to mind. Unhappy fans threw coins onto the floor. "It's always pennies, never quarters," joked the referee.

The only action in the last half came in the final minute when NC State scored on an offensive rebound off a foul shot and then hit two free throws in the last 16 seconds. State won 12-10. Duke had two field goals the entire game; State had four.

We may pride ourselves on our time management, but the truth is that we don't manage time; it manages us. Hurried and harried, we live by schedules that seem to have too much what and too little when. By setting the bedside alarm at night, we even let the clock determine how much down time we get. A life of leisure actually means one in which time is of no importance.

Each second of our life — every bit of the time we have — is a gift from God, who dreamed up time in the first place. We would do well, therefore, to consider what God considers to be good time management. After all, Jesus himself warned us against mismanaging the time we have. From God's point of view, using our time wisely means being prepared at every moment for Jesus' return, which will occur — well, only time will tell when.

I don't fault our strategy not to chase them. Missed foul shots and offensive rebounds beat us.
— Duke Coach Vic Bubas after the 12-10 loss to N.C. State

**We mismanage our time when we fail
to prepare for Jesus' return even though
we don't know when that will be.**

AS YOU SEE IT

Read John 20:11-18.

"Mary stood outside the tomb crying" (v. 11).

From Steve Wojciechowski's perspective, Duke lost the game. Good thing his view wasn't the one that counted.

The Blue Devils had gotten off to a horrendous 0-4 start in the ACC when they took on North Carolina State on Jan. 18, 1996. They desperately needed a win to stop the bleeding and turn the season around.

State led 70-68 with only a few seconds left to play. Coach Mike Krzyzewski had a play called, and senior guard and team captain Chris Collins knew exactly what to do; he just didn't do it. The play called for Collins to pass the ball to sophomore guard Ricky Price. He knew, though, that earlier in the game his man had moved to double-team Price when he got the pass, so Collins faked a pass, saw his man leave him, and took the open shot.

From thirty feet.

Collins' shot "hit the front of the rim, bounced up to the backboard, dropped down, bounced twice more, and dropped through. Duke led 71-70 with 5.5 seconds left.

"Not only did he not do what he was supposed to do, but he almost stepped on my toe," Krzyzewski observed after the game. "But I'll take it."

The game wasn't over, though. The Wolfpack hurried upcourt, and Curtis Marshall tossed up a contested five-foot shot that

BLUE DEVILS

"bounced around and bounced off." The different fates of the two shots turned the season around for the Blue Devils. Duke won eight of its final twelve ACC games and rode the newfound momentum all the way into the NCAA Tournament.

Wojciechowski had a great view of both shots, and from his perspective, everything went State's way. "From my angle, I was sure that Chris's shot was short, and I was sure that Marshall's shot was in," he said. Good thing his perspective was wrong.

Your perspective goes a long way toward determining whether you slink through life amid despair, anger, and hopelessness or stride boldly through life with joy and hope. Mary Magdalene is a good example of the difference a perspective can make in a life

On that first Easter morning, she stood by Jesus' tomb crying, her heart broken, because she still viewed everything through the perspective of Jesus' death. But how her attitude, her heart, and her life changed when she saw the morning through the perspective of Jesus' resurrection.

So it is with life and death for all of us. You can't avoid death, but you can determine how you perceive it. Is it fearful, dark, fraught with peril and uncertainty? Or is it a simple little passageway to glory, the light, and loved ones, an elevator ride to paradise?

It's a matter of perspective that depends totally on whether or not you're standing by Jesus' side when it arrives.

For some people it's the end of the rainbow, but for us it's the end of the finish line.
— *Rower Larisa Healy*

**Whether death is your worst enemy
or a solicitous chauffeur is a matter of perspective.**

BONE TIRED

Read Matthew 11:27-30.

"Come to me, all you who are weary and burdened, and I will give you rest" (v. 11).

I don't remember getting tired. I never thought about it." So spoke George Clark, and if any Duke football player could lay claim to being tired, it would be Clark.

He was a sixty-minute man who ran, passed, kicked, returned kicks, and defended. Clark arrived in Durham in 1944 and almost immediately showed a knack for returning kicks. "We were pretty aggressive on punt returns," he recalled. "I don't ever remember making a fair catch. It just wasn't an option." Against the Demon Deacons of Wake Forest in 1944, Clark returned a punt 95 yards for a touchdown, crediting a block from Tom Davis, who was an All-Southern halfback for three years.

Clark demonstrated his 60-minute versatility in 1945 with a season unimaginable in today's age of specialization, He led the Blue Devils in rushing, scoring, passing yardage, total offense, and kick returns. His one-man offensive season earned him honors as a second-team All-America.

Against Wake that season, he turned in one of the greatest performances in Duke football history. At tailback, he went 69 yards for a touchdown on the first play from scrimmage. On defense, he ended two Deacon threats with a solo tackle and a pass deflection. He broke a 6-6 tie with an 11-yard touchdown run and later broke a 13-13 tie with a 58-yard TD romp.

But the 60-minute man wasn't through. Clark completed a 14-yard pass to John Krisza on fourth down that set up the Devils' final score in the 26-19 win. Clark amassed 214 rushing yards, a school record that stood until Randy Cuthbert broke it against Georgia Tech in 1989. Robert Baldwin and Chris Douglas subsequently broke the record also -- but none of them were tired down by playing defense as George Clark did.

The everyday struggles and burdens of life beat us down. They may be enormous; they may be trivial with a cumulative effect. But they wear us out, so much so that we've even come up with a name for our exhaustion: chronic fatigue syndrome.

Doctors don't help too much. Sleeping pills can zonk us out; muscle relaxers can dull the weariness. Other than that, it's drag on as usual until we can collapse exhaustedly into bed.

Then along comes Jesus, as usual offering hope and relief for what ails us, though in a totally unexpected way. He says take my yoke. Whoa, there! Isn't a yoke a device for work? Exactly. Our mistake is in trying to do it all alone. Yoke ourselves to Jesus, and the power of almighty God is at our disposal to do the heavy lifting for us.

God's strong shoulders and broad back can handle any burdens we can give him. We just have to let them go.

You were just prepared to do whatever the coaches asked you to.
— George Clark on playing 60 minutes

**Tired and weary are a way of life
only when we fail to accept Jesus' invitation
to swap our burden for his.**

YOUNG BLOOD

Read: Jeremiah 1:4-10.

*"The Lord said to me, 'Do not say, 'I am only a child' . . .
for I am with you and will rescue you'" (vv. 7a, 8).*

Shelden Williams expected to have a little time to grow up before the weight of ACC competition and the Duke legacy was laid upon his broad shoulders. He never got the chance.

Williams arrived in Durham in the fall of 2002 for what should have been the senior seasons for Jason Williams, Carlos Boozer, and Mike Dunleavy, three of the standouts of the 2001 national champions. They had all turned pro.

The exodus left Coach Mike Krzyzewski with no choice but to throw his youngsters — including Williams — into the fray right away. When the 2002-03 season opened, Williams and two other freshmen, J.J. Redick and Shavlik Randolph, were starters.

Williams struggled to adjust to the level of the competition. Just how far he had to go became clear when Duke played Maryland in January 2003. "I went in kind of wide-eyed," Williams confessed. "I had never been exposed to that kind of rivalry. . . . I had never seen anything like that in basketball." The Duke-Maryland rivalry was at its zenith. They had met in the Final Four in 2001, and Maryland had followed Duke's title by winning the national championship in 2002.

"It was, in fact, too much for the young Shelden Williams." He got in foul trouble early and scored only three points and had only one rebound. "The biggest reason I didn't play well was that I had not been exposed to that atmosphere," Williams said.

He grew up quickly, had a solid freshman season, and became one of Duke's greatest players ever. He finished his career as the top rebounder and shot blocker in Duke history, was twice the national Defensive Player of the Year, and was All-America.

The jersey of Shelden Williams the man was retired in 2007.

While our mainstream media seem inordinately obsessed with youth, most aspects of our society value experience and some hard-won battle scars. Life usually requires us to spend time on the bench as a reserve, waiting for our chance to play with the big boys and girls. You probably rode some pine in high school. You started college as a lowly freshman. You began work at an entry-level position. Even head football coaches learn their trade as assistants.

Paying your dues is traditional, but that shouldn't stop you from doing something bold right away as Shelden Williams did by becoming an ACC-caliber player as a freshman. Nowhere is this truer than in your faith life.

You may well assert that you are too young and too inexperienced to really do anything for God. Those are just excuses, however, and God won't pay a lick of attention to them when he issues a call. After all, the younger you are, the more time you have to serve.

You're only young once, but you can be immature forever.
— *Former major leaguer Larry Andersen*

Youth is no excuse for not serving God;
it just gives you more time.

HERO WORSHIP

Read 1 Samuel 16:1-13.

"Do not consider his appearance or his height, for . . . the Lord does not look at the things man looks at. . . . The Lord looks at the heart" (v. 7).

DeVon Edwards was an unlikely hero for Duke against N.C. State, but a hero he was.

As the second-string safety behind Jeremy Cash and the backup kick returner to Johnell Barnes, Edwards didn't see much action in Duke's first five games of 2013. He had four tackles and one kickoff return for 12 yards. Then the depth chart imploded; Barnes broke a hand and a starting defender was suspended.

With his playing time increased, Edwards had twelve tackles and returned three kickoffs for 49 yards in the landmark 13-10 upset of Virginia Tech on Oct. 26. (See Devotion No. 91.) It was a solid game. Something better lay dead ahead.

After an off week, the Blue Devils, riding a four-game win streak, hosted N.C. State. Duke led 10-0 at halftime, but the Wolfpack rallied to take a 13-10 lead with 3:45 to go in the third quarter. That's when Edwards suddenly and excitingly emerged as a Blue Devil hero. The redshirt freshman gathered in the kickoff in the end zone and took it 100 yards for a touchdown.

That was heroic enough, but he wasn't through. Duke led only 24-20 after quarterback Brandon Connette scored from the 5 with 3:31 left in the game. On the first snap after the kickoff, Edwards intercepted a State pass and took it 24 yards for a touchdown. He then nabbed a second interception — again on the first play after the kickoff — and returned it 45 yards for a score.

Duke had a 38-20 win, and Edwards, the unlikely hero, joined former Duke cornerback Leon Wright as the only two players in NCAA history to turn back-to-back passes into pick sixes. He was named the national defensive player of the week.

A hero is often thought of as someone who performs brave and dangerous feats that save or protect someone's life. A hero to some is an athlete who does something extraordinary to help his team win as DeVon Edwards did against N.C. State. You figure either situation excludes you.

But ask your son about that when you show him how to bait a hook or throw a football, or your daughter when you show up for her honors night at school. Look into the eyes of those Little Leaguers you help coach.

Ask God about heroism when you're steady in your faith. For God, a hero is a person with the heart of a servant. And if a hero is a servant who acts to save other's lives, then the greatest hero of all is Jesus Christ.

God seeks heroes today, those who will proclaim the name of their hero — Jesus — proudly and boldly, no matter how others may scoff or ridicule. God knows heroes when he sees them — by what's in their hearts.

Nobody foresaw Edwards' explosive performance against N.C. State.
— Writer Danielle Lazarus on Duke's unlikely hero

God's heroes are those who remain steady
in their faith while serving others.

BEST FRIENDS

Read Ecclesiastes 4:9-12.

"If one falls down, his friend can help him up. But pity the man who falls and has no one to help him up!" (v. 10)

The Duke and UNC basketball players were once friends for a day. The result was one of the sloppiest games in the long history of the storied rivalry.

The 1970-71 season was not the greatest for either program. The Blue Devils did go 20-10, but they finished third in the league and were knocked out of the ACC Tournament early on. UNC did little better. As a result, both schools wound up in the NIT.

Duke had a lapse of more than a week without a game between the early exit from the ACC Tournament and the first round of the NIT. Duke coach Bucky Waters figured – probably correctly – that his players would grow tired of practicing against each other. He came up with an unusual solution: He called Dean Smith and asked if he could bring his guys to Chapel Hill to work out with the Heels.

As it turned out, Smith was receptive. He felt that his players needed something to get them over their last-second loss in the conference tournament and thought that the novelty of a practice against Duke just might do it. He told Waters that if the ACC office approved the practice, it was fine with him.

The league honchos said OK, so the archenemies got together in Carmichael Auditorium, and "several formed lifelong friendships from their afternoon together." They ran both offensive and defensive sets against each other and generally had a good time.

As the draw would have it, they wound up facing each other in the NIT semifinals. The result was an "ugly encounter that featured poor shooting and plenty of turnovers." Players from both teams joked with each other about knowing what the other was doing. When a play was called, the defense slid into perfect position since they all knew what was coming. UNC won by six.

Friendships certainly didn't contribute to the quality of play.

Lend her your car or some money. Comfort him when he's down. Talk him out of a bad decision. What wouldn't you do for a good friend?

We are wired for friendship. Our psyche drives us to seek both the superficial company of others that casual acquaintance provides and the more meaningful intimacy that true friendship furnishes. We are perhaps at our noblest when we selflessly help a friend.

So if we wouldn't think of turning our back on our friends, why would we not be the truest, most faithful friend of all by sharing with them the gospel of Jesus Christ? Without thinking, we give a friend a ride, but we know someone for years and don't do what we can to save her from eternal damnation. Apparently, we are quite willing to spend all of eternity separated from our friends. What kind of lousy friend is that?

Friendships, along with love, make life worth living
— *Mike Krzyzewski*

**A true friend introduces a friend
to his friend, Jesus.**

DYNASTY

Read 2 Samuel 7:8-17.

"Your house and your kingdom will endure forever before me; your throne will be established forever" (v. 16).

Blue-Devil fans quite proudly and quite correctly speak of a dynasty when they talk of their basketball teams. The real Duke historical dynasty, however, belongs to the women's tennis program, which at one stretch won fourteen straight ACC titles.

In 2012, the Duke women won their 17th ACC title, becoming the first team in conference history to go 11-0 in league play and then win the ACC Tournament. That simply hearkened back to the years from 1988-2001 when Duke won every ACC title.

When Jane Preyer became head coach of the Duke women in 1985, Clemson ruled the ACC roost. Preyer built her foundation for success on one of the most unusual recruiting coups in sports history. Early on, she secured the O'Reily triplets — Christine, Patti, and Terry — from Ridgewood, N.J. Current Duke coach Jamie Ashworth, who took over the program in 1997 and led the 2009 squad to Duke's first national championship (See Devotion No. 65.), said the O'Reily triplets "put Duke on the map. Jane [Preyer] built the program around them."

That Preyer had snared the O'Reilys away from the likes of tennis powers Stanford and Notre Dame caught the attention of other blue chippers. Susan Sabo, Julie Exum, Monica Mraz, Susan Somerville, and others all soon followed the O'Reilys to Durham.

BLUE DEVILS

The dynasty finally ended in 2002, but not because the Blue Devils had come back to the rest of the league. The goal of other ACC members for years had been to beat Duke, so slowly the teams rose to Duke's level. Now the competition is so fierce that Ashworth has said that an ACC dynasty like Duke's "is not going to happen again. I can't see anyone putting together a run like that. The competition is just too tough."

History teaches us that kingdoms, empires, countries, and even sports programs rise and fall. Dynasties end as events and circumstances conspire and align to snap all winning streaks.

Your life is like that; you win some and lose some. You get a promotion on Monday and your son gets arrested on Friday. You breeze through your annual physical but your dog dies. You finally line up a date with that cutie next door and get sent out of town on business.

Only one dynasty will never end because it is based upon an everlasting promise from God. God promised David the king an enduring line in the appearance of one who would establish God's kingdom forever. That one is Jesus Christ, the reigning king of God's eternal and unending dynasty.

The only way to lose out on that one is to stand on the sidelines and not get in the game.

[Duke's 14-year dynasty] was bigger than the coaches, bigger than the players. The school wanted to be at the forefront and it just fed off itself.
— Duke women's tennis coach Jamie Ashworth

All dynasties and win streaks end except the one
God established with Jesus as its king;
this one never loses and never will.

FAMILY TIES

Read Mark 3:31-35.

"[Jesus] said, 'Here are my mother and my brothers! Whoever does God's will is my brother and sister and mother'" (vv. 34-35).

When the definitive history of the 2010 national championships is written, that account will include stories about the coaches and the players' hard work and dedication. For some of the players, though, that history better talk about family.

For instance, Miles Plumlee couldn't get any playing time at his high school in Indiana. For most families, that wouldn't be such a big deal, but dad had played college ball at Tennessee Tech, mom at Purdue. A grandfather and two uncles had also played college ball. This family took its basketball seriously. So rather than shrug their shoulders, mom and dad sent Miles to a school in North Carolina where the coach gave their son another chance to prove himself. Obviously, he did and wound up providing low-post depth absolutely crucial to the national championship.

Nolan Smith averaged 17.4 points per game for the champs and was the only Duke player "skilled at creating offense off the dribble." Before each game, he looked into the stands and found his mother, who always offered him the same advice: "Go to work." That's what Smith's father used to tell him. His dad was Derek Smith, who played for the 1980 Louisville Cardinals, who won the national championship. Derek died at 34 of an undetected heart defect. Nolan, who was 8, turned to his mother and an older sister for support, calling them his "backbone through everything."

Senior Jon Scheyer led the champs in points per game, assists, free throw percentage, and steals per game. He credited his love for basketball to his dad, who rebounded for him in the driveway but refused to coach him. "He taught me at times, but he was just there for support," Scheyer said.

At Duke, it's still all about family.

Some wit said families are like fudge, mostly sweet with a few nuts. You can probably call the names of your sweetest relatives, whom you cherish, and of the nutty ones too, whom you mostly try to avoid at a family reunion. Like it or not, you have a family, and that's God's doing. God cherishes the family so much that he chose to live in one as a son, a brother, and a cousin.

One of Jesus' more startling actions was to redefine the family. No longer is it a single household of blood relatives or even a clan or a tribe. Jesus' family is the result not of an accident of birth but rather of a conscious choice. All those who profess Jesus Christ as the lord and savior of their lives are members of his family.

What a startling and wonderful thought that is! You have a vastly extended family based on love and a shared belief. You have kinfolk out there you don't even know who stand ready to love you just because you're all part of God's family in Christ.

My family has never been jealous of my success. They have shown true love and commitment to me by being supportive. They shared in it.
— Mike Krzyzewski

For followers of Jesus, family comes not
from a shared ancestry but from a shared faith.

REVELATION

Read Isaiah 53.

*"But he was pierced for our transgressions, he was
crushed for our iniquities; the punishment that brought us
peace was upon him, and by his wounds we are healed"
(v. 5).*

Had Duke Sports Information Director Tom Mickle, who had a
34-year career with the school, not been so successful in his day
job, he might well have moonlighted as a prophet.

Prior to the 1985-86 season, pundits saw a Duke team that was
probably going to be pretty good but clearly wasn't championship
material. The Devils didn't have enough height; they didn't look
particularly physical. So they ranked Duke sixth in the nation but
third in the ACC behind Georgia Tech and UNC.

Perhaps they should have listened to Mickle. In a preseason
magazine, he wrote, "This team is out to prove they are winners.
They want to get into the Final Four and they want to win the
ACC title. I think they can do it." Mickle was right on, for that's
exactly what they did.

Duke was the most experienced team in the country, starting
four seniors — Johnny Dawkins, Mark Alarie, David Henderson,
and Jay Bilas — and junior Tommy Amaker. Dawkins would
leave as Duke's all-time leading scorer; Alarie would also score
more than 2,000 points, the first time in NCAA history any team
had a pair of 2,000-point scorers in the same class. Dawkins

BLUE DEVILS

would become the third Blue Devil — after Dick Groat and Mike Gminski — to have his jersey retired.

Whatever their physical shortcomings, the Devils did one thing better than anyone in the history of college basketball had ever done before: win. Their 37 victories set an NCAA season record.

They won the ACC, losing only twice in the regular season, and advanced to the Final Four (and the championship game), just as Tom Mickle had said.

In our jaded age, we have relegated prophecy to dark rooms where mysterious women peer intently into crystal balls or clasp our sweaty palms while uttering vague generalities. At best, we understand a prophet as someone who predicts future events.

When we open the pages of the Bible, though, we encounter something radically different. A prophet is a messenger from God, one who relays divine revelation to others.

Prophets seem somewhat foreign to us because in one very real sense the age of prophecy is over. In the name of Jesus, we have access to God through our prayers and through scripture. In searching for God's will for our lives, we seek divine revelation for ourselves, not through someone else's vision.

We may speak only for ourselves and not for the greater body of Christ, but we do not need a prophet to discern what God would have us do. We need faith in the one whose birth, life, and death fulfilled more than 300 Bible prophecies.

They will go down as the greatest not-great team ever.
— Jim Valvano's prediction for the 1985-86 Blue Devils

Persons of faith continuously seek a word
from God for their lives.

HEAD GAMES

Read Job 28.

"The fear of the Lord -- that is wisdom, and to shun evil is understanding" (v. 28).

Intentionally hitting an opposing player in the head with the basketball is not a common strategy. It seemed to work, though, for the Blue Devils in a game against North Carolina.

Basketball in the 1930s was a quite different animal from what it is today. For one thing, Duke was a football power, not a basketball power. The 1938 team won the school's first championship, sweeping through the Southern Conference Tournament after four previous losses in the finals. The team was erratic and unpredictable, losing to Davidson by 18 and then whipping Kentucky by 24. Said one sportswriter, "The wisest and most conservative of the sports writers have thrown up their hands in despair in trying to solve Duke's performance."

The Blue Devils put it together, however, in the tournament. They upset N.C. State and Maryland and whipped Clemson in the finals 40-30. Ed Swindell scored 14 points, and Fred "Mouse" Edwards scored 12. Edwards later provided some insight into a different sports era in Durham: "Duke was a football school then, but I think we helped give basketball some recognition."

The strategies employed against an opponent were also often quite different from anything a team tries today. In the early 1930s, Duke practiced a rather unique play in preparation for a game against North Carolina and the Heels' big center, "Tiny" Harper. Bill Werber and Harry Councillor practiced throwing a ball at the head of the Duke center, Joe Crosson, who would duck as the ball neared him. At the beginning of the UNC game, Werber fired the ball at Crosson's head, he ducked and the ball walloped Harper right square in the face. As a writer put it, "the big man was strangely passive the rest of [the] game."

When you talk about using your head, you're speaking of being smart in a manner similar to what Duke employed against UNC. Logic and reason are part of your psyche. A coach's bad call frustrates you, and your children's inexplicable and totally illogical behavior flummoxes you. Why can't people just think things through?

That goes for matters of faith too. Jesus doesn't tell you to turn your brain off when you walk into a church or open the Bible. In fact, when you seek Jesus, you seek him heart, soul, body, and mind. The mind of the master should be the master of your mind so that you consider every situation in your life through the critical lens of the mind of Christ.

With your head *and* your heart, you encounter God, who is, after all, the true source of wisdom. To know Jesus is not to stop thinking; it is to start thinking divinely.

Football is more mental than physical, no matter how it looks from the stands.
— *Pro Hall-of-Fame linebacker Ray Nitschke*

**Since God is the source of all wisdom,
it's only logical that you encounter him
with your mind as well as your emotions.**

DRY RUN

Read John 4:1-15.

*"Everyone who drinks this water will be thirsty again,
but whoever drinks the water I give him will never thirst.
Indeed, the water I give him will become in him a spring
of water welling up to eternal life" (vv. 13-14).*

There's no water in Death Valley. The Blue Devils found enough life, however, to end a drought.

On Oct. 18, 1990, a young Duke football team strolled into Clemson's storied death trap of a stadium with an 11-game losing streak and nary an ACC win since beating Wake Forest 3-0 in 1978. They left with an electrifying 34-17 victory.

"It's been tough times for us," admitted head coach Red Wilson. The times looked to get a whole lot tougher when the Tigers took a 17-10 lead at halftime and appeared to be on their way to a win that would prolong the Duke victory drought.

But freshman quarterback Ben Bennett led the Devils on a 67-yard touchdown drive to start the third quarter, flipping a 5-yard pass to wide receiver Glenn Tillery to complete the drive. Bennett would go on to set seven NCAA, 15 ACC, and 42 school records. His 9,614 career passing yards would be the most in the history of NCAA major-division football.

Four minutes after the Devils tied the game, cornerback Dennis Tabron grabbed his second interception of the game to turn back a Clemson threat. Bennett's offense proceeded to methodically

BLUE DEVILS

drive 84 yards in nine plays with a 13-yard trick play getting the score. Bennett pitched to halfback Mike Grayson, who then lofted a pass back to Bennett.

Then came a game-changing play. With Clemson threatening midway through the fourth quarter, Tabron stepped in front of a Tiger receiver for his third theft of the day. He returned it 87 yards for a 33-17 Duke lead that wrapped up the win.

And ended the drought.

Picking your rocks carefully, you can hopscotch across that river you boated on in the spring. The city's put all neighborhoods on water restriction, and that once-beautiful lawn you so carefully fertilized and seeded is turning a sickly, pale green on its inevitable way toward the unhealthy color of straw. Somebody wrote "Wash Me" on the rear window of your truck.

The sun bakes everything, including the concrete. The earth itself seems exhausted, just barely hanging on. It's a drought.

It's the way a soul looks that shuts God out.

God instilled thirst in us to warn us of our body's need for physical water. He also gave us a spiritual thirst that can be quenched only by his presence in our lives. Without God, we are like tumbleweeds, dried out and windblown, offering the illusion of life where there is only death.

Living water — water of life — is readily available in Jesus. We may drink our fill, and thus we slake our thirst and end our soul's drought — forever.

It is a great, great victory for us.
— Head coach Red Wilson after the win over Clemson

Our soul thirsts for God's refreshing presence.

IN A WORD

Read Matthew 12:33-37.

*"For out of the overflow of the heart the mouth speaks.
The good man brings good things out of the good stored
up in him, and the evil man brings evil things out of the
evil stored up in him" (vv. 34b-35).*

You're darned right Coach Mike Krzyzewski had some words
for his team. After all, they had just been embarrassed by North
Carolina in the finals of the ACC Tournament. The words the
players heard, though, were not what they expected.

The top-seeded Blue Devils had simply fallen apart in the
1991 tourney finals. They lost 96-74 to a UNC team that they had
beaten twice in the regular season. Not surprisingly, therefore, it
was a discouraged bunch of Blue Devils that trudged aboard the
team bus at the Charlotte Coliseum. When Krzyzewski boarded,
he walked to the back of the bus "where the players were waiting
to be seriously chewed out" for their awful play.

But Krzyzewski had led teams to four Final Fours in the past
five years and had learned that it was his job as the head coach to
keep a positive attitude and to set the tone for everyone. So when
he spoke, he delivered words with a purpose.

"We're going to win the national championship," he declared.
The players were so surprised at what they heard that Krzyzewski
repeated it for them. The message was clear: What had just happened was over and done with; it was now NCAA time.

BLUE DEVILS

Krzyzewski's positive words continued an hour later when the pairings for the NCAA Tournament were announced. Duke got a No. 2 seed in the Midwest when they had hoped for a No. 1 seed in the East. "Way to go," Krzyzewski told his team. "Number-two seed in the Midwest. You had a great season."

By the time the team got back on the bus, the gloom from the loss to UNC had been dispelled. The Blue Devils were ready for March Madness to begin. They were ready to go out and win a national title.

These days, everybody's got something to say and likely as not a place to say it. Talk radio, 24-hour sports and news TV channels, late-night talk shows. Talk has really become cheap.

But words still have power, and that includes not just those of the talking heads, hucksters, and pundits on television, but ours also. Our words are perhaps the most powerful force we possess for good or for bad. The words we speak today can belittle, wound, humiliate, and destroy. They can also inspire, heal, protect, and create. Our words both shape and define us. They also reveal to the world the depth of our faith.

We should never make the mistake of underestimating the power of the spoken word. After all, speaking the Word was the only means Jesus had to get his message across – and look what he managed to do.

We must always watch what we say, because others sure will.

You can motivate a player better with kind words than with a whip.
— Legendary college football coach Bud Wilkinson

Choose your words carefully; they are the most powerful force you have for good or for bad.

BE PREPARED

Read Matthew 10:5-23.

"I am sending you out like sheep among wolves. Therefore be as shrewd as snakes and as innocent as doves" (v. 16).

Blue Devil head coach Vic Bubas once prepared his team for a pair of games by employing an unusual tactic at practice.

UCLA was the defending national champion and was ranked No. 1 in the nation as the 1965-66 season began. On Dec. 10 and 11, the Blue Devils hosted the Bruins in back-to-back games. In preparing himself for the game, Bubas spent hours watching the Duke-UCLA championship game of 1964, which the Bruins won 98-83. His biggest problem then became convincing his team of what he had learned from all that study.

The UCLA zone press was such a lethal weapon that it became legendary. Teams so feared it that the Bruins had a significant psychological advantage before they even took the court. Bubas understood that his team's mental approach to that press was just as important as the physical steps they took to attack it.

The coach saw that the UCLA press had been little more than incidental to the 1964 defeat. "Any team that plays the press is going to make it work a few times in any game," he told his team. "Don't get upset when that happens. Expect it."

Bubas then put his team on the floor against the subs, who ran the UCLA zone press. After the regulars broke the press ten straight times, Bubas stopped the practice and pointed out something very obvious they had overlooked: They had been practicing all along against a six-man scrub team.

Thus prepared, the Blue Devils blasted UCLA 82-66 and 94-75. Only six times in 75 tries in the two games were the Bruins able to steal the ball before Duke cleared midcourt.

You know the importance of preparation in your own life. You went to the bank for a car loan, facts and figures in hand. That presentation you made at work went off without a hitch because you practiced. The kids' school play at Thanksgiving suffered no meltdowns because they rehearsed. Knowing what you need to do and then doing what you must to succeed isn't luck; it's preparation.

Jesus understood this, and he prepared his followers by lecturing them and by sending them on field trips. Two thousand years later, the life of faith requires similar training and study. You prepare so you'll be ready when that unsaved neighbor standing beside you at your backyard grill suddenly and unexpectedly asks you about Jesus. You prepare so you will know how God wants you to live. You prepare so you are certain in what you believe when the secular, godless world challenges it.

And one day you'll see God face to face. You certainly want to be prepared for that.

Spectacular achievements are always preceded by unspectacular preparation.

— *Roger Staubach*

Living in faith requires constant study and training, preparation for the day when you meet God face to face.

CELEBRATION TIME

Read Exodus 14:26-31; 15:19-21.

"Miriam the prophetess, Aaron's sister, took a tambourine in her hand, and all the women followed her, with tambourines and dancing" (v. 15:20).

The Blue Devils danced, cried, shouted, hugged, and generally celebrated like the champions they were after they humiliated North Carolina 41-0 to win a share of the 1989 ACC title.

Steve Spurrier's Devils won their seventh straight game and pitched their first shutout since 1978 in stomping the Heels in Chapel Hill and finishing the season at 8-3. The whipping was as thorough as the score would indicate, and the celebration was as raucous as the historic victory would call for.

After soph quarterback Dave Brown completed 33 of 54 passes for 479 yards and three touchdowns against UNC, Duke had set a league single-season total-offense record with 5,519 yards. The three TD tosses all went to flanker Clarkston Hines, who topped 1,000 yards receiving for the third straight year. Hines' 1,149 yards for the year broke his own league record. The touchdown catches upped his NCAA career record to 38 and his school single-season scoring record to 104 points. Contributing to the mayhem Duke inflicted upon Carolina was tailback Randy Cuthbert, who had 116 yards rushing to join Steve Jones (1972) as Duke running backs with more than 1,000 yards in a season.

In the rowdy Blue Devil locker room after the romp, senior linebacker John Howell probably spoke for a whole bunch of Duke players and fans when he said, "We've been waiting all year for this. It all came together today." The 41-point margin was the largest for Duke in the history of the rivalry.

Over a joyous racket, Spurrier told his team that it was the best he'd "ever been on or coached, [or] ever been associated with." He added, "We set high goals and we reached every one of them."

And so the Blue Devils celebrated.

You know what it takes to throw a good party. You start with your closest friends, add some salsa and chips, fire up the grill and throw on some burgers and dogs, and then top it all off with the Duke game on TV.

You probably also know that any old made-up excuse will do to get people together for a celebration. All you really need is a sense that life is pretty good right now.

That's the thing about having Jesus as part of your life: He turns every day into a celebration of the good life. No matter what tragedies or setbacks life may have in store, the heart given to Jesus will find the joy in living.

That's because such a life is spent with quiet confidence in God's promise of salvation through Jesus, a confidence that inevitably bubbles up into a joy that the troubles of the world cannot touch. When a life is shared with Jesus, the troubles and the sadness will pass; the celebration is forever.

Aim high and celebrate that!

— *Marathon runner Bill Rodgers*

**With Jesus, life is one big party because
it becomes a celebration of victory and joy.**

FOOD FOR THOUGHT

Read Genesis 9:1-7.

"Everything that lives and moves will be food for you. Just as I gave you the green plants, I now give you everything" (v. 3).

It must have been the pancakes. That was the only thing that was different about the night Danny Ferry — as teammate Quin Snyder put it — "could have swallowed kryptonite."

As a sophomore in 1986-87, Ferry led the team in scoring and assists and was second-team All-ACC. He led the ACC in scoring his junior season and was the ACC Player of the Year. He then considered turning pro. "In the end, I felt like I'd be missing a lot of fun if I left," he said. "The only reason to go was money, so I decided to stay."

It set him up for what happened on Dec. 10, 1988. As the Blue Devils rolled past overmatched opponents in the early games of the 1988-89 season, Ferry saw little need to score. Thus, he was averaging only 15.4 points per game when Duke played Miami.

Ferry had for some time been asking trainer Max Crowder for some pancakes before a game, a change from the traditional meal of steak and eggs and pasta. "Just once, I wanted pancakes," Ferry said. And this once Crowder gave in and served pancakes.

Maybe it was the pancakes. "I was totally in a zone," Ferry recalled. "My mind was so clear and focused. See ball, catch ball, shoot ball." He had 34 points at halftime. With nine minutes left, he broke Dick Groat's school record of 48 points. Miami stayed close, so Ferry had to keep shooting. He broke David Thompson's ACC record of 57 points with two free throws with 44 seconds left and finished with an ACC-record 58 points on 23 of 26 shooting from the field and 10 of 12 from the foul line. Duke won 117-102.

"Something divine was going on," Snyder said. "Danny could have swallowed kryptonite tonight." Nah. Just pancakes.

Belly up to the buffet, boys and girls, for barbecue, sirloin steak, grilled chicken, and fried catfish with hush puppies and cheese grits. Rachael Ray's a household name; hamburger joints, pizza parlors, and taco stands lurk on every corner; and we have a TV channel devoted exclusively to food. We love our chow.

Food is one of God's really good ideas, but consider the complex divine plan that begins with a kernel and winds up with corn-on-the-cob slathered with butter and littered with salt. The creator of all life devised a downright fascinating and effective system in which living things are sustained and nourished physically through the sacrifice of other living things in a way similar to what Christ underwent to save us spiritually.

Whether it's fast food or home-cooked, practically everything we eat is a gift from God secured through a divine plan in which some plants and/or animals have given up their lives. Pausing to give thanks before we dive in seems the least we can do.

I guess we'll have pancakes more often.
— Max Crowder to Danny Ferry after his record-setting game

God created a system that nourishes us through the sacrifice of other living things; that's worth a thank-you.

COMEBACK KIDS

Read Acts 9:1-22.

*"All those who heard him were astonished and asked,
'Isn't he the man who raised havoc in Jerusalem among
those who call on this name?'" (v. 21)*

Surely there are easier ways to win a basketball game, but on Dec. 30, 1950, the Duke Blue Devils pulled the greatest halftime comeback in NCAA history.

The season was an especially depressing one for everyone associated with the Duke program. Head coach Gerry Gerard had been diagnosed with cancer, and by November he was too sick to continue coaching. He stepped down, and Harold Bradley, the little-known coach at Hartwick College in New York, took over. Bradley would lead the Devils for nine seasons with a 167-78 record. His teams won 20 or more games four times and were the first Duke squads to finish in the top 20. He was the coach when Duke made the move to the new Atlantic Coast Conference.

Despite his eventual success, Bradley got off to a rough start in the consolation game (fifth place) of the Dixie Classic at Reynolds Coliseum in Raleigh. At halftime, Duke trailed Tulane 56-27 and had trailed by 32 points in the first half. They were so far behind that the team's star, Dick Groat (See Devotion No. 90.), confessed, "We never gave that much thought to winning the game. We never had played well in the Dixie Classic."

But Groat went on a tear in the last half, scoring 26 of his game-high 32 points. At one point he scored ten straight points, and as the Devils began to close the gap, the crowd of 12,200 went wild. The Green Wave did not score a single basket in the last 11 minutes of the game.

Groat's basket with just over a minute left tied the game at 72, "and the crowd reaction sounded as though this was the championship game." Duke forced a turnover, and center Dayton Allen hit a layup to give the Devils the 74-72 win. The comeback from the 29-point halftime deficit remains the NCAA's greatest ever.

Life will have its setbacks whether they result from personal failures or from forces and people beyond your control. Being a Christian and a follower of Jesus Christ doesn't insulate you from getting into deep trouble. Maybe financial problems suffocated you. A serious illness put you on the sidelines. Or your family was hit with a great tragedy.

In life, winning isn't about avoiding defeat; that's not going to happen. Rather, it's about getting back up to compete again. It's about making a comeback of your own.

When you avail yourself of God's grace and God's power, your comeback is always greater than your setback. You are never too far behind, and it's never too late in life's game for Jesus to lead you to victory, to turn trouble into triumph. As it was with the Blue Devils on that incredible December night and with Paul, it's not how you start that counts; it's how you finish.

Make it a little respectable.
— Coach Harold Bradley to his players at halftime of the Tulane game

In life, victory is truly a matter of how you finish and whether you finish with Jesus at your side.

DOWNRIGHT CRAZY

Read Luke 13:31-35.

"Some Pharisees came to Jesus and said to him, 'Leave this place and go somewhere else. Herod wants to kill you.' He replied, 'Go tell that fox . . . I must keep going today and tomorrow and the next day'" (vv. 31-33).

Once a Crazy, always a Crazy. If you're lucky.

How the name arose is lost to history, but what is known for certain is that the Cameron Crazies constitute the most famous student body cheering section in the country. They have become legend not just for their fanaticism but for their creativity also.

For instance, in the 1970s Maryland had a forward with bright red hair, a dead-on match for that of Bozo the Clown. Several of the Crazies showed up for the game in clown uniforms with red wigs and floppy shoes. One even jumped into the line behind the player while the Terps were shooting layups.

Television — especially the attention paid to them by the everlastingly exuberant Dick Vitale — has only added to the Crazies' reputation. In 1986, announcer and former Marquette head coach Al McGuire called Cameron a zoo. He then showed up for a game wearing a pith helmet and cracking a whip. Play-by-play announcer Dick Enberg tossed peanuts to the crowd.

The Crazies are able to wreak so much havoc on the opposition because their seats are courtside. Nobody ever sits down — not before, during, or even after a game. Coach Mike Krzyzewski has referred to them as Duke's "Sixth Man" and has purposefully shaped their behavior over the years to cheer for Duke rather than abuse the opponent. A calming influence, if you will.

But still. . . . Several years ago, one Crazy stood as an opponent was shooting a free throw, quickly stripped down to a bathing suit, and proceeded to boogie quite earnestly. The player missed the free throw, and the legend of Speedo Guy was born.

The Cameron Crazies are indeed crazy -- but there's a method to their madness.

What some see as crazy often is shrewd instead. Like the time you went into business for yourself or when you decided to go back to school. Maybe it was when you fixed up that old house. Or when you bought that new company's stock.

You know a good thing when you see it, but conversely you are also shrewd enough to spot something that's just downright crazy. Jesus was that way too. He knew that his entering Jerusalem was in complete defiance of all apparent reason and logic since a whole bunch of folks who wanted to kill him were waiting for him there.

Nevertheless, he went because he also knew that when the great drama had played out he would defeat not only his personal enemies but the most fearsome enemy of all: death itself.

It was, after all, a shrewd move that provided the way to your salvation.

Football is easy if you're crazy.

— *Bo Jackson*

It's so good it sounds crazy -- but it's not: through faith in Jesus, you can have eternal life with God.

DAY 32

HOME FREE

Read 2 Corinthians 5:1-10.

"We . . . would prefer to be away from the body and at home with the Lord" (v. 8).

How good could a *French* basketball player be? Duke women's coach Joanne P. McCallie pretty much wondered the same thing -- and then she saw Allison Vernerey at home.

From Alsace, France, Vernerey played with a national club team in high school, a necessity for a good athlete since French high schools do not have a team sports system comparable to the one offered in American high schools. Her only option after high school would have been to forgo college and turn pro. But Vernerey wanted to play basketball while she continued her studies; that sounded suspiciously like American colleges.

Some of the best women's programs were interested in the 6'5" post player. But her French background raised some questions about her ability to compete at the top collegiate level. After watching some film, McCallie went to Vernerey's small home town near the German border to learn more. There she saw Vernerey's work ethic firsthand and that convinced her.

Her family lives in a remodeled farm house. Vernerey showed the foreigner the barn behind the house where she worked on drills with her father, a pro basketball coach who had trained some members of the French national team. Vernerey practiced every day in that barn. "It was freezing in there," McCallie said.

BLUE DEVILS

The youngster often practiced wearing sweaters and gloves without fingertips, but no matter how cold it got, she worked.

She had some adjustments to make to the faster, more physical American game. A big change for her was speaking English all the time, though she resorted to French when she was upset on the court. After her first semester in 2009, she took a whirlwind trip to Alsace for some home cooking and holiday family time.

Vernerey then returned to her new home to play some American basketball, quite well as it turned out. She saw action in 140 games in her four years, tied for second all-time in Duke history.

Home is not necessarily a matter of geography. It may be that place you share with your spouse and your children, whether it's France or North Carolina. You may feel at home when you return to Durham, wondering why you were so eager to leave in the first place. Maybe the home you grew up in still feels like an old shoe, a little worn but comfortable and inviting.

God planted that sense of home in us because he is a God of place, and our place is with him. Thus, we may live a few blocks away from our parents and grandparents or we may relocate every few years, but we will still sometimes feel as though we don't really belong no matter where we are.

We don't; our true home is with God in the place that Jesus has gone ahead to prepare for us. We are homebodies and we are perpetually homesick.

Everybody's better at home.
— *Basketball player Justin Dentmon*

**We are continually homesick for our real home,
which is with God in Heaven.**

PROMISES, PROMISES

Read 2 Corinthians 1:16-20.

"No matter how many promises God has made, they are 'Yes' in Christ" (v. 20).

Elton Brand played for Duke largely because of what Coach Mike Krzyzewski promised him: nothing.

Brand "was an immediate force" when he arrived at Duke in the fall of 1997. He scored 12 points in his first-ever college game and was leading the team in scoring and rebounding when he broke a bone in his foot on Dec. 27. He missed fifteen games, and the Blue Devils reached the regional finals.

In 1998-99, Brand "was the dominant force in college basketball," which, he said, wasn't as tough as he expected. "The hardest part was Coach K's practices," he said. He led Duke to a 37-2 record and a berth in the championship finals. He was the National Player of the Year. After the season, with Krzyzewski's blessing, he became the first Duke player to turn pro early.

Brand grew up in the housing projects of New York. His mom kept him off the streets by making him join the Boy Scouts and enrolling him in tae kwan do classes. Basketball he picked up on his own. He was a phenomenal high school player, scoring more than 2,000 points and grabbing more than 1,000 rebounds. He came within 20 points of the state scoring record.

Of course, the big schools came calling. His natural inclination was toward the Big East since four players from his AAU team had signed with St. John's. Brand listened to the pitches and the promises, and then he met Krzyzewski. He had repeatedly been promised playing time and a starting position, but Krzyzewski told him, "I don't know what's going to happen. If you deserve to play, you're going to play."

Brand liked the honesty. The Duke tradition didn't hurt either. Duke it was.

The promises you make don't say much about you; the promises you keep tell everything.

The promise to your daughter to be there for her softball game. To your son to help him with his math homework. To your parents to come see them soon. To your spouse to remain faithful until death parts you. And remember what you promised God?

You may carelessly throw promises around, but you can never outpromise God, who is downright profligate with his promises. For instance, he has promised to love you always, to forgive you no matter what you do, and to prepare a place for you with him in Heaven.

And there's more good news in that God operates on a remarkably simple premise: Promises made are promises kept. Thus, you can rely absolutely, without any hesitation or doubt, on God's promises. The people to whom you make them should be able to rely just as surely on your promises.

In the everyday pressures of life, I have learned that God's promises are true.
— *Major leaguer Garret Anderson*

**God keeps his promises just as those
who rely on you expect you to keep yours.**

BRAGGING RIGHTS

Read Job 38.

"Have you ever given orders to the morning, or shown the dawn its place?" (v. 12)

As the sun rose over the world of college basketball Tuesday (April 6, 2010), bragging rights in the Triangle's break rooms and sports bars had shifted, at least for 12 months."

That's because only the day before, the Duke Blue Devils had won the national championship. UNC had fallen "to an inglorious second-place finish in the NIT," and "for Duke fans, their moment on the high end of the 15-501 seesaw was intoxicating."

Kyle Singler scored 19 points, and the Blue Devils' defense held the Butler Bulldogs to 34 percent shooting in the thrilling 61-59 title game. Butler had a shot at the win in the closing seconds with the ball and trailing only 60-59. The Devils forced an off-balance shot that center Brian Zoubek rebounded with only 3.6 seconds left. He was fouled, hit the first, intentionally missed the second, and a half-court shot at the buzzer was wild.

The Blue Devils were national champions for the fourth time, a title that tied Coach Mike Krzyzewski with Kentucky's legendary Adolph Rupp for second place on the all-time list.

The championship was especially sweet for Duke's fans, who had endured two recent titles by UNC. "It's definitely a little sweeter, especially that UNC was the runner-up in the NIT," said a 2007 Duke grad who lived in New York City, home of the NIT.

BLUE DEVILS

Hoarse from his weekend of exhortation, Krzyzewski told a crowd at Cameron Indoor Stadium that joined the team in celebrating the hoisting of a new championship banner, "They're your banners. I really believe we won together this year."

And bragged about it, too, after all the winning was over.

Mankind is forever busy with his achievements and his march toward progress. Cars, planes, computers, Ipods, Oreos. We have been to the moon, virtually eliminated polio, built a tunnel from England to France, concocted weapons capable of destroying our planet, and come up with the flush toilet, chicken nuggets, hair dryers, and Velcro.

We honor each other with prizes and awards for our accomplishments. We name buildings, highways, and bridges after folks who have achieved "great" things. As a species and as individuals, we do like to brag about what we've done.

The truth is, though, that we are nothing compared to God. We brag about space flight; God fashioned the moon, the planets, and the stars and hung them in the heavens he created. Man conducts a symphony; God directs the dawn. Man feebly predicts the weather; God commands it. We struggle to keep a business afloat; God effortlessly manages the universe.

In truth, we have little of which to boast except that God loves us. Now that's worth bragging about!

Let the competition begin; let the glory be God's.
— from the Fellowship of Christian Athletes Competitor's Creed

Boasting and bragging about ourselves
and our accomplishments is one sure way
to make God laugh.

UNBELIEVABLE!

Read Hebrews 3:7-19.

"See to it, brothers, that none of you has a sinful, unbelieving heart that turns away from the living God" *(v. 12).*

Wake Forest with a stout defense. Duke with an offense that had scored ten points all season in the first quarter. So what happened in the first quarter on Nov. 13, 1999, was unbelievable.

What happened is that the Blue Devils set a school record for points scored in a quarter. Wide receiver Scottie Montgomery, who set a Duke record that season for all-purpose yards, ran the opening kickoff back 99 yards, the longest in Duke history. Before the first quarter was over, the homestanding Blue Devils had rolled up an unbelievable 34 points on their way to a 48-35 upset of the Demon Deacons.

After Montgomery's return, the defense held, and Duke raced 61 yards for a touchdown. Kevin Thompson (See Devotion No. 68.) hit wide receiver Richmond Flowers for a touchdown. Safety Darius Clark then grabbed an interception, setting up a 13-yard TD run by Duane Epperson. The game was less than four minutes old and Duke led 20-0. It got worse — or better.

Thompson located Montgomery for a 28-yard touchdown pass that made it 27-0. Linebacker Ryan Stallmeyer recovered a Wake fumble that set up a short Montgomery scoring run. 34-0.

For the day, Montgomery amassed 232 yards for the game,

including three touchdowns. Thompson completed 12 of 19 passes for 128 yards and two touchdowns. Senior tailback Letavious Wilks ran for 128 yards on 20 attempts. The defense had its share of fun, too, with four interceptions and a goal-line stand at the Blue Devil one.

The shellshocked Demon Deacons rallied gamely, but the outcome was decided in that unbelievable first quarter.

Much of what taxes the limits of our belief system has little direct effect on our lives. Maybe we don't believe in UFOs, honest politicians, aluminum baseball bats, Sasquatch, or the viability of electric cars. A healthy dose of skepticism is a natural defense mechanism that helps protect us in a world that all too often has designs on taking advantage of us.

That's not the case, however, when Jesus and God are part of the mix. Quite unbelievably, we often hear people blithely assert they don't believe in God. Or brazenly declare they believe in God but don't believe Jesus was anything but a good man and a great teacher.

At this point, unbelief becomes extremely dangerous because God doesn't fool around with scoffers. He locks them out of the Promised Land, which isn't a country in the Middle East but Heaven itself.

Given that scenario, it's downright unbelievable that anyone would not believe

I couldn't believe it, touchdown after touchdown.
— Duke defensive tackle Chris Combs on the first quarter

Perhaps nothing is as unbelievable as that some people insist on not believing in God or his son.

PASSION PLAY

Read Romans 12:9-21.

"Never be lacking in zeal, but keep your spiritual fervor, serving the Lord" (v. 11).

With just a few weeks left in the 1969 season, Duke basketball head coach Vic Bubas, only 42 years old, "stunned the basketball world" by announcing his retirement. Why did he do it?

Bubas had succeeded Harold Bradley as the Duke head coach. Duke athletic director Eddie Cameron reviewed 135 applications and interviewed ten finalists for the job. He finally went only 25 miles down the road to find Bubas, an assistant at North Carolina State. Legendary State coach Everett Case approved of the hire. He telegraphed Cameron, "Duke has secured an extremely intelligent young man of the highest caliber to direct its program."

Cameron introduced Bubas at a press conference on May 6, 1959. He said simply, "Gentlemen, this is Vic Bubas, our new basketball coach. We hope he is our coach forever."

But he wasn't.

Bubas certainly wasn't under any pressure to resign. In his ten years at the helm, he never had a losing season and had coached the Blue Devils to a 213-67 record and into four NCAA tournaments that included third-place finishes in 1963 and 1966 and a berth in the finals in 1964. But in mid-February, he dropped his bombshell. He called each of his players into his office one at a time and told them exactly why he was leaving.

BLUE DEVILS

Later, he said, "The thought of getting on another plane and chasing another high school kid was just overwhelming. Toward the end I took longer to dress for practice. . . . [I]t wasn't fair to the kids, wasn't fair to the team. It was time to do something else."

Vic Bubas had lost his passion, and he felt his team deserved better than he could deliver. Thus, true to the Blue Devils to the end, he resigned.

What fills your life, your heart, and your soul so much that you sometimes just can't help what you do? We all have a passion for something, whether it's Duke basketball, sports cars, our family, scuba diving, or stamp collecting.

But do we have passion for the Lord? We may well jump up and down, scream, holler, even cry – generally making a spectacle of ourselves – when the Blue Devils win. Yet on Sunday morning, if we go to church at all, we probably sit there showing about as much enthusiasm as we would for a root canal.

Of all the divine rules, regulations, and commandments we find in the Bible, Jesus made it crystal clear which one is number one: We are to love God with everything we have. All our heart, all our soul, all our mind, all our strength.

If we do that, our passion for God will burst forth. We just won't be able to keep ourselves from serving God in the name of Jesus Christ.

[Coach Bubas] told us that he had lost his passion and that it wasn't fair for anyone to continue like that.
— Randy Denton, All-American center in 1971

**The passion with which we serve God reveals
the depth of our relationship with him.**

THE GOOD FIGHT

Read 2 Corinthians 10:1-6.

"For though we live in the world, we do not wage war as the world does. The weapons we fight with are not the weapons of the world" (vv. 3-4a).

Mike Krzyzewski was still a young, unproven coach when he showed the world exactly how much steel he had in his backbone. He took Dean Smith on and didn't flinch.

After an incident at Cameron in 1984, Duke president Terry Sanford wrote what became known as the "Uncle Terry letter." He called on the Cameron Crazies to be creative and not vulgar in their support of the Blue Devils. Naturally, the Crazies saw this as a golden opportunity, responding with signs that read "Welcome, esteemed opponents" and chants of "We beg to differ" after a controversial call.

The first game at Cameron after the Uncle Terry letter was Duke-North Carolina. In the last half, Smith sent a substitute to the scorer's table, but the game resumed before the player got in. A furious Smith "banged the scorer's table, trying to set off the horn and stop play." The referees escorted him back to the bench but didn't hit him with a technical.

After the game, Krzyzewski said what every other coach in the ACC was probably thinking but wouldn't stand up and say. He basically accused the league's officials of employing a double standard: one for North Carolina and one for everybody else.

BLUE DEVILS

Nobody else but Smith, he said, could have gotten away with pointing fingers at the refs and banging on the scorer's table without being assessed a technical foul. "Let's get some things straight around here and quit the double standard that exists in this league, all right?" the coach concluded.

Three days later, the coach who "had publicly put a dunce cap on Dean Smith's head" got a five-year contract extension.

Violence is not the Christian way, but what about confrontation? Following Jesus' admonition to turn the other cheek has rendered many a Christian meek and mild in the name of obedience. But we need to remember that the Lord we follow once bullwhipped a bunch of folks who turned God's temple into a flea market.

With Christianity in America under attack as never before, we must stand up for and fight for our faith. Who else is there to stand up for Jesus if not you? Our pretty little planet — including our nation — is a battleground between good and evil. We are far from helpless in this fight because God has provided us with a powerful set of weapons. Prayer, faith, hope, love, the Word of God itself and the Holy Spirit — these are the weapons at our command with which to vanquish evil and godlessness.

We are called by God to use them, to fight the good fight, not just in our own lives but in our nation and in our world.

When you're part of a team, you stand up for your teammates.
— Yogi Berra

'Stand up, Stand up for Jesus'
is not an antiquated hymn
but is a contemporary call to battle for our Lord.

BAD IDEA

Read Mark 14:43-50.

"The betrayer had arranged a signal with them: 'The one I kiss is the man; arrest him and lead him away under guard'" (v. 44).

Anthony Dilweg once had an idea that was so bad that an assistant coach told him he would never play football for Duke again.

Dilweg arrived at Duke in the fall of 1984 largely because he looked to a time beyond football. He was one of the nation's top prep quarterbacks until he suffered a knee injury. "That made me think of life without football," he said. "Suddenly that scholarship offer from Duke [because of the school's academics] seemed a lot more attractive." He was redshirted, but then in 1985 he became the team's punter, a job he kept for four years.

Dilweg saw the combination of punter and back-up quarterback as a natural for a fake punt, but coach Steve Sloan didn't think so. Finally, in the season's last game against North Carolina, Dilweg had what turned out to be a horrendously bad idea. He tried an unauthorized fake punt. It didn't work, and the coaches were so furious that one told Dilweg his days as a football player at Duke were over.

After that game, though, Sloan was fired and was replaced by Duke's former offensive coordinator, Steve Spurrier. After a film session, Spurrier put his arm around Dilweg's shoulder and told him how much he admired the fake punt that failed. "You were trying to make a play to help your team win. I like that," the new coach said.

Still, Dilweg sat behind Steve Slayden until he was a fifth-year senior in 1988. In his one season, though, he flourished under Spurrier, leading Duke to a 7-3-1 season by shattering the ACC record with 3,824 passing yards, a Blue-Devil record that still stands. He was the league's Player of the Year.

That sure-fire investment you made from a pal's hot stock tip. The expensive exercise machine that now traps dust bunnies under your bed. Blond hair. Telling your wife you wanted to eat at the restaurant with the waitresses in little shorts. They seemed like pretty good ideas at the time; they weren't.

We all have bad ideas in our lifetime. They provide some of our most crucial learning experiences. Anthony Dilweg, for instance, learned from his one attempt not to get into the habit of trying spontaneous fake punts.

Some ideas, though, are so irreparably and inherently bad that we cannot help but wonder why they were even conceived in the first place. Almost two thousand years ago a man had just such an idea. Judas' betrayal of Jesus remains to this day one of the most heinous acts of treachery in history.

Turning his back on Jesus was a bad idea for Judas then; it's a bad idea for us now.

Now I've done it. How do I get out of this mess?
— Anthony Dilweg after his failed fake punt

**We all have some pretty bad ideas
during our lifetimes, but nothing equals
the folly of turning away from Jesus.**

TEARS IN HEAVEN

Read Isaiah 25:1-9.

"The Sovereign Lord will wipe away the tears from all faces" (v. 8b).

There are tears in basketball — and sometimes they even come from the coach.

Christian Laettner led Duke to four consecutive Final Fours and two national championships and was the National Player of 1992. While he was at Duke, he encountered some tears from a totally unexpected source. Laettner's freshman season of 1988-89 ended with a 95-78 loss to Seton Hall in the national semifinals. After the game, the team returned to their hotel, and Coach Mike Krzyzewski called a team meeting in his suite.

As Coach K started speaking, he looked across to his seniors, John Smith, Danny Ferry, and Quin Snyder. Krzyzewski couldn't help himself; he started crying. Laettner, sitting on the floor, "seemed bewildered," Krzyzewski recalled. "Maybe he had never seen an adult cry before [except for his mother, who cried when he chose Duke over UNC]. It was difficult for me to speak."

Finally, Krzyzewski just gave up trying to talk. He told his players, "You guys go be with your families. . . . We're staying through the championship game to celebrate our season."

With that, the team dispersed, leaving their teary-eyed coach. Later that evening about 11 p.m., someone knocked on Coach K's door. It was Laettner, who, Krzyzewski noted, "was eighteen years old and had just lost the biggest game of his life." Why was he there? To check on his coach. "Coach, are you all right?" he asked. Krzyzewski told him he was, but Laettner sat down next to him and again asked, "Are you okay, Coach?" As he left the room, he asked a third time, "Are you sure you're okay, Coach?"

Only after three reassurances from his once-tearful coach did Laettner leave the room.

When your parents died. When a friend told you she was divorcing. When you broke your collarbone. You cry. Crying is as much a part of life as are breathing and indigestion. Usually our tears are brought on by pain, sorrow, or disappointment.

But what about when your child was born? When Duke beats North Carolina? When you discovered Jesus Christ? Those times elicit tears too; we cry at the times of our greatest, most overwhelming joy.

Thus, while there may be tears in Heaven, they will only be tears of sheer, unmitigated, undiluted joy. The greatest joy possible, a joy beyond our imagining, must occur when we finally see Christ. If we shed tears and lose our composure when Duke wins a game, can we really believe that we will stand dry-eyed and calm in the presence of Jesus?

What we will not shed in Heaven are tears of sorrow and pain; those God will wipe away forever.

I will always remember his caring for me. It gave me one of the best feelings I have ever had as a coach, better than any victory.
— Mike Krzyzewski on Christian Laettner's concern for him

**Tears in Heaven will be like everything else there:
a part of the joy we will experience.**

DAY 40

A LONG SHOT

Read Matthew 9:9-13.

"[Jesus] saw a man named Matthew sitting at the tax collector's booth. 'Follow me,' he told him, and Matthew got up and followed him" (v. 9).

Most of the time Duke enters the ACC Tournament as one of the favorites. If ever the Blue Devils were long shots to win even a game, though, it was in 1960.

Duke was only 12-10 for the season and 7-7 in the conference. North Carolina had trounced them three times: by 22, 25, and 26 points. They had lost twice to Wake Forest, by 17 and 19 points. The squad closed out the season by losing five of its last seven, including a 75-50 drubbing by the Heels. "The Devils obviously looked like anything but champions."

They played well, though, in the opening round and upset South Carolina 82-69. Their reward? A fourth meeting with North Carolina. Before the game Duke coach Vic Bubas told his team, "We have been manhandled three times, so there is no reason for you to be tight this time. To the contrary, I want you to be loosey-goosey. Just go out there and play basketball."

That's exactly what the Blue Devils did. Behind 30 points from junior Carroll Youngkin and 17 from junior Howard Hurt, the long shots shocked North Carolina 71-69, which earned the Blue Devils yet another dubious reward. Waiting for them in the tournament finals was Wake Forest. It didn't seem to matter; the long shots surprised the Demon Deacons, too, 63-59, with junior Doug Kistler scoring 22 points.

The unlikely ACC champions went on and buried Princeton 84-60 and upset St. Joseph's 58-56 in the NCAA Tournament. The long shots to win a single game in the conference tournament came within one win of making the Final Four.

Matthew the tax collector was another long shot, though in his case it involved becoming a confidant of the Son of God. While we may not get all warm and fuzzy about the IRS, our government's revenue agents are little like Matthew and his ilk. He bought a franchise, paying the Roman Empire for the privilege of extorting, bullying, and stealing everything he could from his own people. Tax collectors of the time were pretty much "despicable, vile, unprincipled scoundrels."

And yet, Jesus picked this lowlife to join his inner circle, saying only two words to him: "Follow me." Jesus knew that this long shot would make an excellent disciple.

It's the same with us. While we may not be quite as vile as Matthew was, none of us can stand before God with our hands clean and our hearts pure. We are all impossibly long shots to enter God's Heaven. That is, until we do what Matthew did: get up and follow Jesus.

When you get down to realism, it would have been incredible if we had gone to San Francisco [and the Final Four].
— *Coach Vic Bubas*

Only through Jesus does our status change from being long shots to enter God's Kingdom to being heavy favorites.

FEAR FACTOR

Read Matthew 14:22-33.

"[The disciples] cried out in fear. But Jesus immediately said to them: 'Take courage! It is I. Don't be afraid'" (vv. 26-27).

Dave Brown was a bundle of fears and nerves. "My knees were shaking before the game," he admitted. He found a way to calm his fears quickly: He threw a touchdown pass on the first play of the game.

On Nov. 4, 1989, the 5-3 Blue Devils found themselves facing Wake Forest without starting quarterback Billy Ray, sidelined by a sore shoulder suffered the week before. The game was crucial since Duke was very much in the hunt for the ACC title. Their fate lay in the hands of a virtually untested sophomore who hadn't thrown a pass in anger since the Virginia game six weeks earlier.

Brown learned for sure on the eve of the game that he was the starter. That started the shaky knees and the inflamed nerves, but Brown also learned that the first play of the game was to be a deep pass. That knowledge cued the worry. "I was worried all morning," he said. "What if it's intercepted?"

So the nervous quarterback who feared an interception trotted onto the field after the kickoff with that first play. He quickly put his fears to rest by firing a 76-yard touchdown bomb to record-setting flanker Clarkston Hines. Coach Steve Spurrier helped his rookie QB out by disguising the pass with a run formation that featured two tight ends. Brown faked to tailback Randy Cuthbert and delivered the strike to a wide-open Hines.

With his fears and nerves calmed, Brown proceeded to throw for 444 yards, hitting 24 of 36 passes, as the Blue Devils romped to a 52-35 blasting of the Demon Deacons. The last time Brown and Hines connected in the game was even more spectacular than the first: a 97-yard touchdown, the longest in Duke history.

As it turned out, Brown had absolutely nothing to be afraid of.

Some fears are universal; others are particular. Speaking to the Rotary Club may require a heavy dose of antiperspirant. Elevator walls may always give you the distinct impression that they're closing in on you. And don't even get started on being in the dark with spiders and snakes during a thunderstorm.

We all live in fear, and God knows this. Dozens of passages in the Bible urge us not to be afraid. God isn't telling us to lose our wariness of oncoming cars or big dogs with nasty dispositions; this is a helpful fear God instilled in us for protection.

What God does wish driven from our lives is a spirit of fear that dominates us, that makes our lives miserable and keeps us from boldly doing what we should for him, such as sharing our faith. In commanding that we not be afraid, God reminds us that when we trust completely in him, we find peace that calms our fears.

I think you're not a human being unless you have doubts and fears.
— Mike Krzyzewski

You have your own peculiar set of fears,
but they should never paralyze you
because God is greater than anything you fear.

MAKE NO MISTAKE

Read Mark 14:66-72.

*"Then Peter remembered the word Jesus had spoken to
him: 'Before the rooster crows twice you will disown me
three times.' And he broke down and wept" (v. 72).*

Two mistakes by the game's dominant programs took them out
of the running for one of college basketball's greatest players.

Alana Beard is both a Duke and a basketball legend, displaying
her awesome and jersey-retiring talents from 2000-04 in Durham.
(See Devotion No. 6 for a list of Beard's accomplishments.) When
she was in high school and considering college ball, Duke wasn't
in the mix. Until a couple of the big guys made mistakes.

Beard grew up in Shreveport, La., playing basketball on a dirt
court with her parents and older siblings. When she was in high
school, her team won four state championships. In her final game,
she scored a state-record 48 points.

While other colleges came calling early on, Tennessee and Connecticut were late catching on because they relied heavily on AAU
tournaments and all-star camps for national recruiting. Beard's
AAU team had only a limited budget and didn't play in a national
tournament until after Beard's junior season.

Beard's heart was set on Tennessee. In 1999, her AAU coach
sent a videotape to Knoxville of Beard scoring 24 points against
a team of all-stars two years older than she. The tape was mislaid
amid a stack of others, and that mistake doomed UT's chances.

BLUE DEVILS

UConn? They didn't even try. An associate coach mistakenly relied on some faulty intelligence that said Beard wanted to stay in Louisiana. The Huskies never even called.

And Duke? Head coach Gail Goestenkors saw Beard play for a Mississippi AAU team and scribbled herself a note that said, "Best player I've ever seen." That was no mistake.

It's distressing but it's true: Like recruiters and Simon Peter, we all make mistakes. Only one perfect man ever walked on this earth, and no one of us is he. Some mistakes are just dumb. Like locking yourself out of your car or falling into a swimming pool with your clothes on. Other mistakes are more significant. Like heading down a path to addiction. Committing a crime. Walking out on a spouse and the children.

All these mistakes, however, from the momentarily annoying to the life-altering tragic, share one aspect: They can all be forgiven in Christ. Other folks may not forgive us; we may not even forgive ourselves. But God will forgive us when we call upon him in Jesus' name.

Thus, the twofold fatal mistake we can make is ignoring the fact that we will die one day and subsequently ignoring the fact that Jesus is the only way to shun Hell and enter Heaven. Make no mistake, we absolutely must get this one right; all of eternity is at stake.

Coach Pat Summitt glares at me every time [Alana Beard's] name comes up.
> — *Tennessee assistant coach Mickie DeMoss*

**Only one mistake we make sends us to Hell
when we die: ignoring Jesus while we live.**

NO PLACE LIKE HOME

Read Joshua 24:14-27.

*"Choose for yourselves this day whom you will serve. . . .
But as for me and my household, we will serve the Lord"
(v. 15).*

The Duke Blue Devils once had the home-field advantage — in the Rose Bowl!

Duke Stadium was the first facility used on the new Duke University campus a mile or so to the west of the original Durham site. On Oct. 5, 1929, the Blue Devils hosted Pittsburgh in the new stadium, nine months before the opening of the hospital on July 1, 1930, and a year before the beginning of the 1930-31 school year. Fans had to be bused to the new stadium. That the facility and football even existed was rather remarkable since Trinity College had reinstated football only in 1920 after a 24-year ban. In July 1967, the stadium was renamed in honor of Wallace Wade, who coached the Blue Devils for sixteen seasons to a 110-36-7 record.

Wade's 1941 Blue Devils were Southern Conference champions with a perfect 9-0 record. They averaged 34.5 points per game, the second highest total in the country, and were a natural pick for a slot in the Rose Bowl against Oregon State, the champions of the Pac 10.

One rather severe problem existed, however. In the wake of the Japanese attack on Pearl Harbor in December 1941, large crowds were not allowed to assemble on the West Coast; the Rose Bowl

BLUE DEVILS

was perhaps the biggest gathering of all. Duke officials extended an invitation to have the game played in Durham, and the head honchos at the Rose Bowl took them up on their offer, the only time the game has not been played in Pasadena. How much the home-field helped the Blue Devils is uncertain since the Beavers won a 20-16 thriller.

In honor of the displaced 1942 Rose Bowl, rose bushes courtesy of the Tournament of Roses Committee flank the bust of Wallace Wade at the stadium entrance.

You enter your home to find love, security, and joy. It's the place where your heart feels warmest, your laughter comes easiest, and your life is its richest. It is the center of and the reason for everything you do and everything you are.

How can a home be such a place?

If it is a home where grace is spoken before every meal, it is such a place. If it is a home where the Bible is read, studied, and discussed by the whole family gathered together, it is such a place. If it is a home that serves as a jumping-off point for the whole family to go to church, not just on Sunday morning and not just occasionally, but regularly, it is such a place. If it is a home where the name of God is spoken with reverence and awe and not with disrespect and indifference, it is such a place.

In other words, a house becomes a true home when God is part of the family.

Sure, the home field is an advantage, but so is having a lot of talent.
— Dan Marino

A home is full when all the family members —
including God — are present.

THE LEADER

Read Matthew 16:13-19.

"You are Peter, and on this rock I will build my church, and the gates of Hades will not overcome it" (v. 18).

With one question and the answer he got, Mike Krzyzewski knew he had found the leader his team needed to win a national championship.

In preparing his teams for an upcoming season, Krzyzewski always identified at least one player who would be the leader, the one who would "lift everybody else to a higher level of performance and achievement." As the 2000-01 season neared, Coach K believed he had found that person.

Krzyzewski and his wife, Mickie, met with senior Shane Battier and freshman Jason Williams over lunch in Hawaii prior to the season. The players were helping the Olympic team prepare; the coach and his wife were attending a reunion of the 1992 Olympic "Dream Team," for which Krzyzewski was an assistant coach.

When Williams stepped away for a moment, Coach K asked Battier a loaded question: "How's Jason doing?" The senior's reply was direct: "He's the best player here. No doubt about it."

After the two players left, the coach said to his wife, "Well, *he's* rock solid." She thought he meant Williams, but he was referring to Battier, whose answer had impressed him. "Did you hear how honestly he responded about his teammate — the one who, no doubt, will give him the most competition for attention this year?"

BLUE DEVILS

Krzyzewski pointed out that Battier could have been noncommittal or deflected the conversation to himself — but he didn't.

"That's our senior leader," Coach K said. "Honest. No jealousy. Rock solid."

That senior leader led his team all the way to the title.

Every aspect of life that involves people — every organization, every group, every project, every team — must have a leader. If goals are to be reached, somebody must take charge.

Even the early Christian church was no different. Jesus knew this, so he designated the leader in Simon Peter, who was, in fact, quite an unlikely choice to assume such an awesome, world-changing responsibility. In *Twelve Ordinary Men*, John MacArthur described Simon as "ambivalent, vacillating, impulsive, unsubmissive." Hardly a man to inspire confidence in his leadership skills. Yet, Peter became, according to MacArthur, "the greatest preacher among the apostles" and the "dominant figure" in the birth of the church.

The implication to be drawn from Peter's life for your own life is both obvious and unsettling. You may think you lack the attributes necessary to make a good leader for Christ. But consider Simon Peter, an ordinary man who allowed Christ to rule his life and became the foundation upon which the Christian church was built.

A leader has to be positive about all things that happen to his team.
Look at nothing in the past as failure.
— *Mike Krzyzewski*

**God's leaders are men and women
who allow Jesus to lead them.**

GREAT EXPECTATIONS

Read John 1:43-51.

"'Nazareth! Can anything good come from there?'
Nathanael asked" (v. 46).

Sometimes, even at Duke, expectations for the men's basketball team have to be tempered with a dose of reality. Such was the case for the 1993-94 squad — and then all they did was reach the national championship game.

The team's most glaring weakness was the absence of a point guard. What Duke did have was All-America senior Grant Hill. Moving Hill certainly solved the problem at point guard, but it left a gaping hole at power forward. "We'll be experimenting until the season is over," Coach K said about his lineup.

As the ACC schedule began, Krzyzewski settled for a while on freshman Jeff Capel and sophomore Chris Collins at the guard spots, which allowed him to move Hill back to the frontcourt some. "Ball handling is done by committee," Collins said.

Yet another problem for the Devils was depth -- or the lack of it. As the season progressed, only seven players saw much action. More and more the team came to rely on Hill. "I'm still working on the play where [Hill] can pass the ball to himself," Krzyzewski said after a particularly impressive Hill performance.

The lack of depth and the long season wore both Hill and his teammates down some. Duke shot only 36 percent in an upset loss to Virginia in the ACC semifinals. With expectations doused

BLUE DEVILS

by the loss, the Blue Devils revived them again by advancing to the NCAA finals before losing to Arkansas. "We went absolutely as far as we could," Krzyzewski said.

It was the school's sixth Final Four in seven seasons, a run that has known no peer in the era of tournaments with 64-and-more teams and balanced regionals. The Blue Devils of 1993-94 had overcome their problems to raise expectations for Duke basketball yet again.

The blind date your friend promised would look like Brad Pitt or Jennifer Aniston but resembled a Munster. Your vacation that went downhill after the lost luggage. Often your expectations are raised only to be dashed. Sometimes it's best not to get your hopes up; then at least you have the possibility of being surprised.

Worst of all, perhaps, is when you realize that you are the one not meeting others' expectations. The fact is, though, that you aren't here to live up to what others think of you. Jesus didn't; in part, that's why they killed him. But he did meet God's expectations for his life, which was all that really mattered.

Because God's kingdom is so great, God does have great expectations for any who would enter, and you should not take them lightly. What the world expects from you is of no importance; what God expects from you is paramount.

I thought we did a lot for a team that didn't have a point guard, a power forward or much depth.
— Grant Hill on the 1993-94 Blue Devils

**You have little if anything to gain from meeting
the world's expectations of you; you have all
of eternity to gain from meeting God's.**

CALLING IT QUITS

Read Numbers 13:25-14:4.

"The men who had gone up with him said, 'We can't attack those people; they are stronger than we are'" (v. 13:31).

As the losses and the sacks mounted, he could have quit, could have transferred. Instead, he stayed; by the time he left, he had become the greatest quarterback in Duke football history.

When head coach David Cutcliffe arrived at Duke and watched film of his new team, what he saw repeatedly was his quarterback getting knocked to the ground. "He impressed me that he was still here," Cutcliffe said.

That quarterback was Thaddeus Lewis. After a 1-23 record and 85 sacks his first two seasons, no one could have blamed him for leaving. "The easy way out would have been transferring," he said. The losses certainly got to him. "I broke down crying one time," he admitted, "because I'm a competitor." But he never seriously thought about leaving; he stayed and fought, always confidently picking himself up and completing another pass.

Lewis wound up completing a bunch of passes. From the time he became a starter in 2006 in the second college game of his life, until the time he finished up in 2009, Lewis set or tied 54 school records. He set Duke career records for pass completions (877), pass attempts (1,510), passing touchdowns (67), and passing yards (10,065), the latter the second-most in ACC history.

The tough quarterback who wouldn't quit actually started out as the crybaby of the family. An older brother toughened him up by teaching Lewis to fight, a necessary survival trait in a neighborhood "where words often turned to fisticuffs."

And Thaddeus Lewis never quit fighting, even after he left the tough streets of home and took to the tough fields of college football. His refusal to quit carried him to Duke football glory.

Remember that time you quit a high-school sports team? Bailed out of a relationship? Walked away from that job with the goals unachieved? Sometimes quitting is the most sensible way to minimize your losses, so you may well at times in your life give up on something or someone.

In your relationship with God, however, you should remember the people of Israel, who quit when the Promised Land was theirs for the taking. They forgot one fact of life you never should: God never gives up on you.

That means you should never, ever give up on God. No matter how tired or discouraged you get, no matter that it seems your prayers aren't getting through to God, no matter what — quitting on God is not an option.

That's because God is always about the divine business of preparing a blessing for you. In his time, he will bring it to fruition — if you don't quit on him.

Where [Thaddeus] Lewis is from, you don't cut and run when hit. You stay at Duke and fight out of a losing tradition.
— *Sportswriter Edward G. Robinson III*

Whatever else you give up on in your life, don't give up on God; he will never ever give up on you.

AS A RULE

Read Luke 5:27-32.

"Why do you eat and drink with tax collectors and 'sinners'?" (v. 30b)

The Duke coaches took a good hard look at the NCAA rule book, spotted a loophole, and took advantage of it to gain their young basketball team some extra practice and playing time.

The 2002-03 squad had only two returning starters. The only senior had played just one season in Durham. What was on the squad were freshmen, six of them. Clearly, the Blue Devils would take their licks early on until this bunch of youngsters got some experience. Until the coaching staff spent some time examining the rule book.

They discovered something that no one else had ever noticed before in that they could find no rule prohibiting a team from taking a pre-season trip overseas if no classes were missed. Some schools regularly took foreign trips in the summer, but this one was different. It was in the fall; therefore, freshmen could go. Without the six rookies, Duke didn't even have enough bodies to play. The trip, therefore, was invaluable for the freshmen, who played four games in London against pro teams. Not only that, the team was allowed to begin practice for the trip on Sept. 28. They had ten days of practice more than two weeks before anybody else could start working out.

The excursion drew some criticism, but it was clearly legal.

Other coaches agreed they would have done the same thing if they had known they could have. In April 2004, the NCAA closed the loophole, decreeing that no fall overseas trips could be made.

The advantage had been gained, though. Instead of starting off slowly, Duke jumped out to a 12-0 start — all because the coaches studied the rules.

You live by rules others set up. Some lender determined the interest rate on your mortgage and your car loan. You work hours and shifts somebody else established. Someone else decided what day your garbage gets picked up and what school district your house is in.

Jesus encountered societal rules also, including a strict set of religious edicts that dictated what company he should keep, what people, in other words, were fit for him to socialize with, talk to, or share a meal with. Jesus ignored the rules, choosing love instead of mindless obedience and demonstrating his disdain for society's rules by mingling with the outcasts, the lowlifes, the poor, and the misfits.

You, too, have to choose when you find yourself in the presence of someone whom society deems undesirable. Will you choose the rules or love? Are you willing to be a rebel for love — as Jesus was for you?

The truth is that many people set rules to keep from making decisions. Not me. I don't want to be a manager or a dictator. I want to be a leader.
— Mike Krzyzewski

Society's rules dictate who is acceptable and who is not, but love in the name of Jesus knows no such distinctions.

PAIN RELIEF

Read 2 Corinthians 1:3-7.

"Just as the sufferings of Christ flow over into our lives, so also through Christ our comfort overflows" (v. 5).

Whatever else you could say about Blue Devil guard Tate Armstrong, he could certainly play with pain. He once played most of a game and all of an overtime with a broken wrist. He scored 33 points.

Armstrong spent most of his first two seasons at Duke on the bench with assorted injuries and illnesses. Coach Bill Foster was convinced that if Armstrong were in better shape, he could shake off his nagging injuries and become a better player. He suggested Armstrong take up distance running. So during the 1975 summer before his junior season, Armstrong went home to Houston and worked up to running twenty miles a day in the Texas heat. "We didn't expect that," Foster said. "Tate willed himself into a great player. I never had a player work harder."

The results were immediate and spectacular. Armstrong shot better than 52 percent from the field in 1975-76, though many of his shots were outside today's three-point line. "We told Tate to keep shooting until his right arm fell off, and then we'd talk about getting him a new arm," Foster said.

In 1976-77, Duke started out 10-1 and was receiving votes for the Top 20 for the first time since 1971. In a road game at Virginia, however, Armstrong fell hard on his right wrist. He kept on playing despite intense pain.

When trainer Max Crowder tried to examine the wrist at half-time, Armstrong refused. "I yelled at Max and actually threw a bucket of ice against the wall at halftime," Armstrong said. "I was so angry, but we were going to win that game. They were going to have to shoot me to get me off the court."

So Armstrong played on, leading Duke to an 82-74 win in over-time. But as he had feared, the wrist was broken; his career at Duke was over. Without their leader and scorer, Duke finished 14-13, a disappointment after the great start.

Since you live on Earth and not in Heaven, you are forced to play with pain as Tate Armstrong did against Virginia. Whether it's a car wreck that left you shattered, the end of a relationship that left you battered, or a loved one's death that left you tattered -- pain finds you and challenges you to keep going.

While God's word teaches that you will reap what you sow, life also teaches that pain and hardship are not necessarily the result of personal failure. Pain in fact can be one of the tools God uses to mold your character and change your life.

What are you to do when you are hit full-speed by the awful pain that seems to choke the very will to live out of you? Where is your consolation, your comfort, and your help?

In almighty God, whose love will never fail. When life knocks you to your knees, you're closer to God than ever before.

I knew right away I had broken it. The pain was intense.
— Tate Armstrong on his broken right wrist

When life hits you with pain, you can always
turn to God for comfort, consolation, and hope.

THE INTERVIEW

Read Romans 14:1-12.

"We will all stand before God's judgment seat. . . . So then, each of us will give an account of himself to God" (vv. 10, 12).

When Eddie Cameron interviewed for a coaching position at Duke, his truthful answer to one question cost him the job.

"The coaching change that eventually would make Duke the basketball powerhouse that it remains today" was made in 1928 when Cameron, only 26, was named the basketball head coach. He coached for 14 years and had a 226-99 record. He was Duke's winningest coach until Mike Krzyzewski surpassed his win total in 1990. He had only one losing season, a 10-12 record in 1938-39.

Cameron was also an assistant football coach. When head coach Wallace Wade went into active duty with the U.S. Army after the 1942 Rose Bowl, Cameron gave up the basketball team to assume the dual duties of football coach and athletic director. His teams went 25-11-1. He remained as athletic director until 1972. Shortly before he retired after 46 years at Duke, the basketball building was renamed Cameron Indoor Stadium in his honor.

Cameron pretty much flunked his original job interview with Duke. He stayed on as an assistant coach at Washington & Lee for one year after playing football there and graduating in 1924. When he interviewed for a football assistant's job at Duke, the university's vice-president looked at the 23-year-old and asked simply, "You're too young to coach football, aren't you?" Cameron gave an honest answer. "I don't know," he said.

The two men then decided upon an unusual tactic. Cameron would coach a year at a military academy in West Virginia to gain some experience before coming to Duke. They each lived up to the unusual agreement, and in 1926, Cameron became the freshman football coach at Duke. The rest is the stuff of Duke legend -- despite that rather unsuccessful interview.

You know all about job interviews even if you've never had one in which one question basically sandbagged you. You've experienced the stress, the anxiety, the helpless feeling. You tried to appear calm and relaxed, struggling to come up with reasonably original answers to banal questions and to cover up the fact that you thought the interviewer was a total geek. You told yourself if they turned you down, it was their loss, not yours.

You won't be so indifferent, though, about your last interview: the one with God. A day will come when we will all stand before God to account for ourselves. It is to God and God alone – not our friends, not our parents, not society in general – that we must give a final and complete account.

Since all eternity will be at stake, it sure would help to have a surefire reference with you. One – and only one – is available: Jesus Christ.

I hereby apply for the head coaching job at Auburn.
— Shug Jordan's complete job application in 1951

You will have one last interview – with God –
and you sure want Jesus there with you
as a character witness.

TEST CASE

Read James 1:2-12.

"Blessed is the man who perseveres under trial, because when he has stood the test, he will receive the crown of life that God has promised to those who love him" (v. 12).

Duke's track coaches were skeptical about what they were hearing about a baseball player named Dave Sime, so they gave him a test. What they discovered was one of the greatest athletes in Duke and perhaps in American history.

Sime came to Durham in 1954 on a scholarship baseball coach Clarence "Ace" Parker had put together. In the fall of 1955, he ran some with the track team to stay in shape for baseball. To everyone's surprise, including his own since he had never run track before, Sime was the fastest guy on the track. Word got over to Duke track coach Bob Chambers and his assistants, Red Lewis and Al Buehler. They decided to see for themselves, so they tested Sime by putting a stopwatch on him over 100 yards.

The track was in monumentally bad shape because a convoy of trucks was grinding over it regularly to maintain the football field. Still, Sime ran a 9.8, only .2 of a second off the school record. What the coaches had uncovered to their amazement was a talent Buehler — who had a 45-year career at Duke — once called "the greatest athlete in ACC history."

Only a few months later, Sime set a world record in the 220-yard low hurdles. At the same meet against UNC, he won the 100-

and the 220-yard dashes with times only .1 second off the world records. He finished second in the broad jump, third in the discus, and second in the high jump -- all in one afternoon.

Sime soon became a national sensation. *Sports Illustrated* called him "Superman in Spikes." Only an injury kept him out of the 1956 Olympics; he won the Silver Medal in the 100 meters in 1960 and was on the winning 4x100-meter relay team that was disqualified. After the Olympics, he gave up athletics.

And it all started when he aced a test.

Life often seems to be one battery of tests after another: high-school and college final exams, college entrance exams, the driver's license test, professional certification exams. They all stress us out because they measure our competency, and we fear that we will be found wanting.

But it is the tests in our lives that don't involve paper and pen that often demand the most of us. That is, we regularly run headlong into challenges, obstacles, and barriers that test our abilities, our persistence, and our faith.

Life itself is one long test, which means some parts are bound to be hard. Viewing life as an ongoing exam may help you keep your sanity, your perspective, and your faith when troubles come your way. After all, God is the proctor, but he isn't neutral. He even gave you the answer you need to pass with flying colors; that answer is "Jesus."

Experience is a hard teacher because she gives the test first, the lesson afterward.
— *Former major league pitcher Vernon Law*

Life is a test that God wants you to ace.

KEEPING THE PEACE

Read Hebrews 12:14-17.

"Make every effort to live in peace with all men and to be holy" (v. 14).

The Blue Devils didn't lose the fight, but they may well have lost the season.

On Feb. 4, 1961, Duke and UNC met for the first time when both schools were ranked in the top five. Duke, 15-1, was No. 4; the Tar Heels were 14-2 and ranked No. 5.

The day after athletic director Eddie Cameron announced he had been hired as Duke's new head basketball coach, Vic Bubas went to New York and convinced high-school star Art Heyman to switch from North Carolina to Duke. Heyman was the first of a succession of All-Americas Bubas lured to Duke. Following him were Jeff Mullins (1964), Jack Marin ('66) (See Devotion No. 59.), Bob Verga ('67), and Mike Lewis ('68).

In 1961, as a sophomore, Heyman joined seniors Doug Kistler, Carroll Youngkin, and Howard Hurt on the varsity. He was the star in the Feb. 4 showdown with the Tar Heels, rolling up 36 points. He made two free throws with fifteen seconds left to play that clinched the win by giving Duke an 80-75 lead.

But then Heyman fouled Carolina guard Larry Brown with nine seconds left. Brown took offense at the hard foul, and the two squared off and threw punches. The foul happened right in front of the Carolina bench, and the Heels poured onto the court.

BLUE DEVILS

The Blue Devil players followed suit; some Duke students also felt compelled to take to the floor and contribute to the melee.

Police broke up the fight in a couple of minutes, and Duke won 81-77. But ACC Commissioner Jim Weaver banned Heyman and two UNC players from the remainder of the ACC games, and "Duke was never the same after that." The Devils dropped five of their last eleven games and lost to Wake Forest in the ACC finals.

Perhaps you've never been in a brawl or a public brouhaha to match that of Art Heyman and his Duke teammates, but maybe you retaliated when you got one elbow too many in a pickup basketball game. Or maybe you and your spouse or your teenager get into it occasionally, shouting and saying cruel things. Or road rage may be a part of your life.

While we do seem to live in a more belligerent, confrontational society than ever before, fighting is still not the solution to a problem. Rather, it only escalates the whole confrontation, leaving wounded pride, intransigence, and simmering hatred in its wake. Actively seeking and making peace is the way to a solution that lasts even as it heals broken relationships and wounded hearts.

Peacemaking is not as easy as fighting, but it is certainly much more courageous and a lot less painful. It is also exactly what Jesus would do.

No matter what the other fellow does on the field, don't let him lure you into a fight. Uphold your dignity.
— Legendary Alabama football coach Frank Thomas

Making peace instead of fighting takes courage and strength; it's also what Jesus would do.

IN THE BAD TIMES

Read Philippians 1:3-14.

"What has happened to me has really served to advance the gospel. . . . Because of my chains, most of the brothers in the Lord have been encouraged to speak the word of God more courageously and fearlessly" (vv. 12, 14).

Steve Wojciechowski arrived in Durham expecting to be a part of the winningest basketball program in the country. Instead, he experienced the worst times the Blue Devils had undergone in more than a decade.

When the point guard from Baltimore signed with Duke in the fall of 1993, he was joining "one of the most solid and successful programs in the country." He watched eagerly from high school as Grant Hill led Duke to its seventh Final Four in nine seasons. He expected more good times.

It started out that way. The 1994-95 team got off to a fast 9-2 start. Wojciechowski was soon starting and contributing, on his way to having the best assist/turnover ratio in Duke history. But Coach Mike Krzyzewski's health was crumbling. (See Devotion No. 87.) Chris Collins, who was named Coach K's associate head coach in 2008, said, "This guy was always our rock. Now all of a sudden, he's breaking down." Krzyzewski had to leave the team.

The rock broke down and so did the team. Almost overnight, the season fell apart; the Blue Devils lost 16 of their last 20 games. Wojciechowski was a casualty of the mayhem; he went from starting to disappearing at the end of the bench.

From the depths that constituted Wojchiechowski's freshman season, however, the Blue Devils rose again and so did the point guard. He started his last three seasons and helped restore Duke to its rightful place among the nation's elite programs. As a senior in 1998, Wojciechowski led Duke to a 32-4 season and the first of nine straight Sweet 16 Finishes. The bad times were over.

Loved ones die. You're downsized. Distance has grown between your spouse and yourself, and you never even realized it was happening. Your biopsy looks cancerous. Hard, tragic times are as much a part of life as breath.

This applies to Christians too. Christianity is not the equivalent of a Get-out-of-Jail-Free card, granting us a lifelong exemption from either the least or the worst pain the world has to offer. While Jesus promises us he will be there to lead us through the valleys, he never promises that we will not enter them.

The question therefore becomes how you handle the bad times. You can buckle to your knees in despair and cry, "Why me?" Or you can hit your knees in prayer and ask, "What do I do with this?"

Setbacks and tragedies are opportunities to reveal and to develop true character and abiding faith. Your faithfulness — not your skipping merrily along through life without pain — is what reveals the depth of your love for God.

I felt hurt because who wants to play on a team losing that many games.
— Steve Wojciechowski on his freshman season at Duke

Faithfulness to God requires faith even in —
especially in — the bad times.

RECIPE FOR DISASTER

Read Luke 21:5-11, 25-28.

"There will be great earthquakes, famines and pestilences in various places, and fearful events and great signs from heaven" (v. 11).

The new coach's "first foray on the recruiting trail [was] nothing less than a disaster." That new coach was Mike Krzyzewski.

Coach K's first team, the 1980-81 squad, went 17-10 and landed in the NIT. Unfortunately, it wasn't a young team since most of the success could be attributed to seniors Gene Banks and Kenny Dennard. Vince Taylor was the last "quality holdover" from Bill Foster's regime.

Part of the problem for Krzyzewski was that he came to Duke from West Point, a background that "didn't prepare him for the world of big-time recruiting." That first year, it showed. Coach K went after the talent he needed, but "the inexperienced duke coach couldn't close the deal." The 1981-82 team went 10-17.

After the season, Krzyzewski took to the recruiting trail with a vengeance that ensured the results would be different this time. His recruitment of 6-foot-9 Californian Jay Bilas illustrates how tenacious he was. He would fly across the country just to watch Bilas in a pick-up game and then hop on a red-eye back to Carolina. Sometimes, Bilas recalled, he and his teammates couldn't get in the gym, so they'd play outdoors. Coach K "would sit on the front steps of . . . portable classrooms . . . just watching us play. He was all by himself. Nobody knew who he was."

Krzyzewski didn't miss this time. He successfully recruited four players who became starters: Bilas; Mark Alarie, a first-round NBA draft choice; swingman David Henderson; and Johnny Dawkins, "the recruit who would make his program."

Recruiting was never a disaster again for Coach K.

We live in a world that seems to be either struck by one disaster after another or is the home of several ongoing and seemingly permanent disasters. Earthquakes virtually obliterate an entire nation; volcanoes erupt and change the climate; children around the world starve to death every day. Floods devastate cities and shatter lives; oil pollutes our oceans and seashores. Can we even count the number of wars that are going on at any one time all across the planet?

This apparently unending litany of disaster is enough to make us all give up hope. Maybe – but not for the followers of Jesus Christ. The truth is that Jesus' disciples should find reassurance of their ultimate hope in the world's constant disasters because this is exactly what Jesus said would happen.

These disasters indicate that the time of our redemption is drawing near. How near is up to God to decide. Nevertheless, this is a season of hope and great promise for those of the faith.

The minute you think you've got it made, disaster is just around the corner.
— *Joe Paterno*

**Jesus told us what to do when disaster
threatens to overwhelm us and our world:
'Stand up and lift up your heads.'**

JUST IMAGINE

Read Revelation 1:4-18.

"His face was like the sun shining in all its brilliance. When I saw him, I fell at his feet as though dead" (vv. 16b-17a).

Imagine, if you will, a college football team that goes 8-2, wins the conference championship, is ranked 14th in the nation — and turns down a bowl bid. That's exactly what the Blue Devils of 1962 did.

Duke didn't sneak up on anybody; they were ranked eighth in the nation in the first AP poll. The team was experienced; linemen and Duke Sports Hall of Fame inductees Jean Berry and Art Gregory, lineman Dick Havens, quarterback Walt Rappold, and running back Mark Leggett had been together for five seasons. "By this point we had practiced and played together so much that we didn't have to say anything. We just knew," Berry said.

The Blue Devils lost only to Southern Cal and Georgia Tech. They expected an invitation to the Gator Bowl, but bowl officials dawdled for a week, and when the invitation finally came, the Blue Devils overwhelmingly voted not to go.

Several factors played into the unusual decision. Berry said some of the players didn't want to repeat the holiday experience of the Cotton Bowl two seasons before. "You gave up your holidays, you couldn't eat much during the holidays, you were away from home," he said. Athletic director Eddie Cameron suggested that

BLUE DEVILS

the Gator Bowl wasn't prestigious enough for Duke. Some players were miffed at the bowl for waiting a week. "We would have gone if [coach Bill] Murray" had asked us," Berry said. "But he didn't."

So the Blue Devils voted not to go to a bowl, a decision that's hard to imagine in today's game where everybody goes bowling.

We are blessed (or cursed) with generally active imaginations. We can, for instance, quite often imagine what someone or some place looks like from a description. That includes our lord and savior. Most if not all of us probably have in our minds an image of what Jesus the man looked like. Some things, however, are beyond our imagining until we experience them or see them in person. Slavery. The birth of our child. Krispy Kreme donuts. Life in prison.

And add to that list the glorified Jesus. When Jesus ascended to Heaven, he assumed his rightful place in glory right there with God the Father, another unimaginable sight. In so doing, Jesus, the gentle man who drew children close to him and wept over the death of a friend, achieved a radiant splendor the likes of which we can't really imagine despite John's attempt to describe the scene for us. He isn't Jesus the man anymore.

Imagine this: One day we will see the glorified Jesus face to face; we won't have to imagine what he looks like anymore. What we can't imagine is the depth of the joy that sight will bring us.

It was the right decision. There were a lot of factors. It just wasn't right.
— Duke Hall of Fame lineman Jean Berry on the '62 bowl decision

The glorified Jesus is unimaginable
as is the joy we will experience
when we come into his presence.

GOOD SPORTS

Read Titus 2:1-8.

"Show integrity, seriousness and soundness of speech that cannot be condemned, so that those who oppose you may be ashamed because they have nothing bad to say about us" (vv. 7b, 8).

Christian Laettner's jersey was retired; Bobby Hurley made it back into the lineup after an injury. All in all, the night was special for the Blue Devils and their fans. It became even more wonderful when they offered up an unusual act of sportsmanship by honoring a player from the opposing team.

Less than seven minutes into the Carolina game of Feb. 5, 1992, Bobby Hurley, the NCAA's all-time assists leader, flipped a pass to Thomas Hill for the layup that broke the school assist record. "I heard something pop," Hurley would say about the play. The "something" was his foot; he broke it, and the injury sent him to the sidelines until the Virginia game of Feb. 26.

The night started off in grand style as the crowd "went bonkers" when Laettner's No. 32 was retired in pre-game ceremonies. Then the students "cheered themselves hoarse" when Hurley came out with the team for warmups. The crowd's biggest roar of the night came with 13:56 left in the half when Hurley went into the game.

On cue, Laettner responded with 32 points and a season-high 13 rebounds, and Hurley played 26 minutes and had nine assists. Duke won 76-67 and clinched the ACC regular-season title on the way to the national championship.

With seconds left in the game, Virginia's Bryant Stith broke the school record for career points and then had to be helped off the floor with a severe cramp. Stith had played for Coach Mike Krzyzewski in the world championships, and after the game ended, the Duke coach presented Stith with the game ball. The sportsmanship was the perfect ending to a great night.

One of life's paradoxes is that many who would never consider cheating on the tennis court or the racquetball court to gain an advantage think nothing of doing so in other areas of their life. In other words, the good sportsmanship they practice on the golf course or on the Monopoly board doesn't carry over.

Instead, they play loose and free with the truth, cut corners, abuse others verbally, run roughshod over the weaker, and cheat pretty much whenever they can to gain an advantage on the job or in their personal relationships.

But good sportsmanship is a way of living, not just of playing. Shouldn't you accept defeat without complaint (You don't have to like it.); win gracefully without gloating; treat your competition with fairness, courtesy, generosity, and respect? That's the way one team treats another in the name of sportsmanship. That's the way one person treats another in the name of Jesus.

One person practicing sportsmanship is better than a hundred teaching it.

— *Knute Rockne*

Sportsmanship — treating others with courtesy, fairness, and respect — is a way of living, not just a way of playing.

DAY 56

ANGER MANAGEMENT

Read James 1:19-27.

"Everyone should be quick to listen, slow to speak and slow to become angry, for man's anger does not bring about the righteous life that God desires" (vv. 19-20).

Clemson was matching the Blue Devils point for point, but then the Tigers made a serious mistake. They got Duke angry.

The 1998-99 Blue Devils went 37-2, losing in the NCAA finals 77-74 to Connecticut. All five starters — Elton Brand, Shane Battier, Chris Carrawell, Trajan Langdon, and William Avery — made All-ACC, the only time that has ever happened. Brand was both the ACC and the National Player of the Year, and both Brand and Langdon were All-America. The Devils went undefeated in ACC play.

Thus, they were expected to have little trouble with the Tigers in the last home game of the season. But nobody told Clemson, and the game was tied at 30 with under eight minutes to go in the half. That's when the Tigers woke up the sleeping Duke giant.

Langdon, the team's senior captain, was flattened with a forearm blow that left him on the floor bleeding from the mouth. He lay on the court for several minutes and eventually had to be helped to the locker room.

"Seeing Trajan down turned on a switch for us," Carrawell said. "We went off. It was show no mercy."

Clemson scored to take the lead, but then, as Carrawell put it,

Duke "went off" and showed no mercy. They scored and scored and scored some more. Before Clemson scored again, Duke had ripped off 26 straight points and turned the game into a rout.

Langdon received some stitches, went back into the game, and scored 17 points. Duke won 92-65.

The moral of the story was clear: Don't make Duke mad.

Our society today is well aware of anger's destructive power because too many of us don't manage our anger very well. Anger is a healthy component of a functional human being until – like other normal emotions such as fear, grief, and worry — it escalates out of control. Anger abounds among the faithful when the Blue Devils lose; the trouble comes when that anger intensifies from annoyance and disappointment to rage and destructive behavior.

However, anger not only has those practical consequences but spiritual ones, too. Its great spiritual danger occurs when anger is "a purely selfish matter and the expression of a merely peevish vexation at unexpected and unwelcome misfortune or frustration" as when Duke commits a turnover in the last seconds of a game. It thus interferes with the living of the righteous, Christ-like life God intends for us.

Our own anger, therefore, can incur God's wrath; making God angry can never be anything but a perfectly horrendous idea.

My captain was lying on the floor, bleeding. If I'm not emotional, some-body else needs to sit in the chair.
— Mike Krzyzewski when asked about his angry reaction to the foul

Anger becomes a problem when it escalates
into rage and interferes with the righteous life
God intends for us.

LESSON LEARNED

Read Psalm 143.

"Teach me to do your will, for you are my God" (v. 10).

Johnny Dawkins knew exactly why the Blue Devils were able to storm into the championship game of the 1986 NCAA Tournament: They learned a lesson from their first-round game.

Dawkins finished his career in Durham in 1986 as the school's all-time leading scorer, a record that held up until J.J. Redick broke it in 2006. He was named one of the ACC's fifty greatest players, was Duke's first consensus two-time first-team All-America, and was the National Player of the Year as a senior in 1986.

That '86 team set an NCAA record with 37 wins and won the ACC regular-season and tournament titles. Naturally, the team earned a No. 1 seed in the NCAA Tournament, which guaranteed the Blue Devils a first-round blowout. Funny thing about that.

The opponent was Mississippi Valley State, which had no intentions of rolling over for the mighty Blue Devils. Dawkins put it succinctly: "They played us well." As a largely passive Greensboro crowd looked on in dismay, State led 44-37 with 12 minutes left to play. "I can remember thinking in disbelief that we were losing to this team," Dawkins said.

So Dawkins did something about it. In a five-minute span, he scored 16 of his game-high 27 points. Duke rallied for an 85-78 win over a team that Dawkins insisted had no business being a No. 16 seed. "I still believe that this day," he said years later.

BLUE DEVILS

After that scare, one of the closest calls a No. 1 seed has ever had in the first round, the Blue Devils were unstoppable until the finals with wins over Old Dominion, DePaul, Navy with David Robinson, and Kansas. Dawkins attributed that strong run to what the Devils learned from their close call against Mississippi Valley State. "That game was a wakeup call for us," he said." The team couldn't win on its laurels. "This NCAA Tournament was its own entity."

Learning about anything in life requires a combination of education and experience. Education is the accumulation of facts that we call knowledge; experience is the acquisition of wisdom and discernment, which add purpose and understanding to our knowledge.

The most difficult way to learn is through trial and error: dive in blindly and mess up. The best way to learn is through example paired with a set of instructions: Someone has gone ahead to show you the way and has written down all the information you need to follow.

In teaching us the way to live godly lives, God chose the latter method. He set down in his book the habits, actions, and attitudes that make for a way of life in accordance with his wishes. He also sent us Jesus to explain and to illustrate.

God teaches us not just how to exist but how to live. We just need to be attentive students.

It's what you learn after you know it all that counts.
— John Wooden

To learn from Jesus is to learn what life is all about and how God means for us to live it.

MEMORY LOSS

Read 1 Corinthians 11:17-29.

"[D]o this in remembrance of me" (v. 24).

Devin Pierce kept a photograph on his dorm desk to remind him of a man he didn't remember but who nevertheless served to inspire him every day.

Pierce was a four-year letterman at fullback for Duke from 1997-2000. His last two years he was the starter. When Pierce was a freshman in high school, his mother refused to let him try out for the football team, so he came up with an unusual form of persuasion. He asked his classmates to sign a petition asking his mom to change her mind. It worked. She gave in, never realizing her son was the petition's instigator.

Pierce's football success led to some scholarship offers, but he turned them all down to pursue the Air Force Academy. That's because of the photograph that eventually sat on his desk at Duke. It was a picture of his father, an Air Force pilot for years who then became a commercial pilot. When Devin was 3, his dad was killed in a crash caused by wind shear.

While the younger Pierce didn't really remember his dad, his mother made sure her son knew about his father: that "he was devoted to his family, carried his Bible with him wherever he traveled, and was an honor student at North Carolina A&T."

Thus, Pierce hoped to emulate his father as an Air Force pilot, but the Academy turned him down because of problems with asthma. "I think the Lord had other things in mind for me," he said about his disappointment. "Things couldn't have worked out better."

That's because the Air Force football coach took a personal interest in Pierce's situation and made arrangements for Pierce to visit Duke. He immediately liked what he saw and accepted a scholarship from Coach Fred Goldsmith. And always, in Durham, the picture reminded him of the man who inspired him to do his very best.

Memory makes us who we are. Whether our memories are dreams or nightmares, they shape us and to a large extent determine our actions and reactions. Alzheimer's is terrifying because it steals our memory from us and in the process we lose ourselves. We disappear.

The greatest tragedy of our lives is that God remembers. In response to that memory, he condemns us for our sin. On the other hand, the greatest joy of our lives is that God remembers. In response to that memory, he came as Jesus to wash even the memory of our sins away.

Through memory, we encounter revival. At the Last Supper, Jesus instructed his disciples and us to remember. In sharing this unique meal with fellow believers and remembering Jesus and his actions, we meet Christ again not just as a memory but as an actual living presence. To remember is to keep our faith alive.

He was everything I want to be.

— *Devin Pierce on his father*

We remember Jesus,
and God will not remember our sins.

WEATHERPROOFED

Read Nahum 1:3-9.

"His way is in the whirlwind and the storm, and clouds are the dust of his feet" (v. 3b).

Duke landed one of its greatest basketball players ever because of the weather.

Duke head coach Vic Bubas regarded Jack Marin as the best all-around player of his era. As a sophomore in 1963-64, Marin played behind senior Jeff Mullins. The Blue Devils went 25-6 and advanced to the NCAA Finals, which UCLA won. In that game, Marin scored 16 points and had ten rebounds.

Marin was a starter as a junior and earned first-team All-ACC honors. The 1965-66 team, Marin's senior season, earned Duke's first-ever No. 1 national ranking and won both the ACC regular-season and tournament titles. Marin was first-team All-ACC again and second-team All-America. Duke lost to Kentucky 83-79 in the NCAA semifinals with Marin scoring 29 points.

From Western Pennsylvania, Marin was a nationally known prospect by the end of his junior year in high school. The family pressure was on Marin to attend Pitt, though he was looking for any excuse to avoid making a commitment. He found it when the Pitt coach failed to show for a Saturday morning meeting with Marin and his dad. "If he's not there to meet us on time, we're probably not that important to him," Marin suggested. "We just picked up and drove off." It turned out that the coach had missed the meeting because he had failed to change his clocks to daylight time. The visit was never rescheduled.

With Pitt out, Duke and Michigan became the favorites. Marin visited Duke "on a spring day when it was beautiful — about 70 degrees, blue skies." Accustomed to walking to practice on cold snow, Marin called the weather "a revelation" — especially when he visited Michigan, "and it was cold and foggy and drizzling." The contrast in weather locked up the decision.

A thunderstorm washes away your golf game or the picnic with the kids. Lightning knocks out the electricity just as you settle in at the computer. A tornado interrupts your Sunday dinner and sends everyone scurrying to the hallway. A hurricane cancels your beach trip.

For all our technology and our knowledge, we are still at the mercy of the weather, able only to get a little more advance warning than in the past. The weather answers only to God. Rain and hail will fall where they want to; the elements are totally inconsiderate of something as important as a Duke athletic event.

We stand mute before the awesome power of the weather, but we should be even more awestruck at the power of the one who controls it, a power beyond our imagining. Neither, however, can we imagine the depths of God's love for us, a love that drove him to die on a cross for us.

A significant part of my decision had to do with weather.
— Jack Marin on his decision to attend Duke

The power of the one who controls the weather is
beyond anything we can imagine,
but so is his love for us.

LIVE ACTION

Read James 2:14-26.

"Faith by itself, if it is not accompanied by action, is dead"
(v. 17).

Basketball teams are often inspired by trash-talking opponents whose words become bulletin board material before a game. Duke, however, was once motivated by the ill-conceived and obviously brain-dead comments of a team the Devils had just defeated.

"In the past, I've just packed a handkerchief and that's about it." So spoke Duke head coach Bill Foster about the 1978 ACC Tournament. He was speaking an exaggerated but sad truth: The Blue Devils had not won a league title since 1966. "But," Foster went on, "this time I packed for the whole week, and so did the team."

This time, the Blue Devils needed the extra clothes. They beat Clemson, Maryland, and Wake Forest to win the title and set up a game against 24-6 Rhode Island in the NCAA Tournament. With 17 seconds left, Mike Gminski hit a free throw for a 63-62 win that sent the Devils to a game against Penn. The Quakers led 64-56 but made a crucial mistake by switching to a spread offense to make it easier to drive against Duke's zone. That worked fine until the guards reached Gminski, who swatted away practically everything Penn threw at the basket. Duke went on an 18-2 run over seven minutes and won 84-80.

Next up was Villanova, and that's when all the trash talking started. Strangely, it didn't come from Villanova but from Penn. The Penn coach said Villanova would win by six. One Quaker with a problem with his short-term memory said, "I don't think Gminski's especially intimidating. . . . Every time we got two on one, we'd beat him." He apparently had forgotten Gminski's seven blocked shots. Another Penn player, who likewise seemed to have forgotten who won the game, piped up: Duke's "awfully slow afoot. That's going to hurt them against Villanova."

Inspired by the talk, Duke never let Villanova lead. The Devils led 21-6 early and by 21 at halftime. With a 90-72 romp, Duke was on its way to the Final Four.

Talk is cheap. Consider your neighbor or coworker who talks without saying anything, who makes promises she doesn't keep, who brags about his own exploits, who can always tell you how to do something but never shows up for the work.

How often have you fidgeted through a meeting, impatient to get on with the work everybody is talking about doing? You know – just as the 1978 Blue Devils did and the Penn players apparently forgot – that speech without action just doesn't cut it.

That principle applies in the life of a person of faith too. Merely declaring our faith isn't enough, however sincere we may be. It is putting our faith into action that shouts to the world of the depth of our commitment to Christ. Just as Jesus' ministry was a virtual whirlwind of activity, so are we to change the world by doing.

Jesus Christ is alive; so should our faith in Him be.

Our guys were really ticked off about all that stuff that's been written.
— Duke assistant coach Lou Goetz on Penn's trash talk

Faith that does not reveal itself in action is dead.

MIRACLE PLAY

Read Matthew 12:38-42.

"He answered, 'A wicked and adulterous generation asks for a miraculous sign!'" (v. 39)

It will forever be known as the 'Miracle Minute.'"

On Jan. 27, 2001, in College Park, Maryland led Duke 89-77 with only 1:15 left to play. ESPN conceded a Maryland win and named a Terrapin as the Player of the Game. With 61 seconds left, the Maryland students started chanting, "Over-rated" at the second-ranked Blue Devils.

The Terps outplayed Duke for most of the game. Despite the legendary final minute, a play key to the game's outcome occurred in the last 1.4 seconds of the first half. Maryland missed a shot and the half had apparently ended. But the shot had missed the rim, a shot-clock violation, and the refs put 1.4 seconds back on the clock. Mike Dunleavy heaved the ball the length of the floor, and Jason Williams banked home a shot at the buzzer.

It looked as though it wouldn't matter as Maryland led 90-80 with 61 seconds left and Duke out of time outs. But then came the miracle. Williams made a layup with 54 seconds left. 90-82. He then stole the inbounds pass and nailed a three with 49 seconds left. 90-85. Andre Buckner committed a foul before the clock started, and Maryland missed both free throws. Duke hurried downcourt, and Williams buried another trey at 40 seconds. He had scored eight points in 14 seconds. 90-88.

After a Maryland timeout, Nate James stole the inbounds pass. He was subsequently fouled on a tip-in attempt and hit both free throws. 90-90 with 22 seconds left. In 39 seconds, the Blue Devils had erased a 10-point lead. When Maryland missed a shot at the buzzer, the game went into overtime, and Duke won 98-96.

"They had done an extraordinary thing," Coach Mike Krzyzewski later wrote about his team's miraculous comeback.

Miracles – like Duke's "Miracle Minute" – defy rational explanation. Escaping with minor abrasions from an accident that totals your car – that's one. Or recovering from an illness that the medical experts had declared was terminal.

Underlying the notion of miracles is that they are rare instances of direct divine intervention that reveal God. But life shows us quite the contrary, that miracles are anything but rare.

Since God made the world and everything in it, everything around you is miraculous. Even you are a miracle. Your life thus can be mundane, dull, and ordinary, or it can be spent in a glorious attitude of childlike wonder and awe. It depends upon whether or not you see the world through the eyes of faith. Only through faith can you discern the hand of God in any event; only through faith can you see the miraculous and thus see God.

Jesus knew that miracles don't produce faith, but rather faith produces miracles.

We're going to come back and we're going to win. Everybody's going to be talking about this game forever.
        — Nate James during the time out with about a minute left

**Miracles are all around us,
but it takes the eyes of faith to see them.**

CASH AND CARRY

Read 1 Peter 1:13-25.

"It was not with perishable things such as silver or gold that you were redeemed from the empty way of life handed down to you from your forefathers, but with the precious blood of Christ" (vv. 18-19).

Redemption was four years in the making, but it arrived on May 31, 2010, when Duke's men's lacrosse team beat Notre Dame to win the national championship.

Sophomore long-stick midfielder C.J. Costabile scored off a face-off in overtime for the 6-5 win that finished a 16-4 season and the school's first-ever national title. Notre Dame held a 5-4 lead with 8:44 left when midfielder Justin Turri scored to gain the tie.

This wasn't just any old national title, though. This was one four years in the making that involved not only gaining credence on the field but redemption in the hearts and minds of everyone associated with the program.

When John Danowski was hired in July 2006 to coach the team, the young men who played the game at Duke "were trapped in a dangerous siege almost no one could have imagined." The siege began in March when criminal charges were lodged against three team members. In the aftermath, the remainder of the season was cancelled, the head coach was forced out, and a clamor arose for the sport to be dropped.

The players were eventually exonerated, but the damage had

been done to men's lacrosse at Duke. "The scars on the program lingered to the extent that there was good reason to question whether the appetite for competition could be restored." The answer came quickly; the 2007 team reached the title game, losing by a goal.

Then in 2010 came "Duke's bid for the ultimate redemption." It was achieved that May afternoon with "the loudest possible statement about the spirit of [the] program."

In our capitalistic society, we know all about redemption. Just think rebate or coupons. To receive the rebates or the discount, though, we must redeem them; we must cash them in.

"Redemption" is a business term; it reconciles a debt, restoring one party to favor by making amends as was the case with the Duke lacrosse team, which won the title for all the players since 2006. In the Bible, a slave could obtain his freedom only by a redeemer's paying money. In other words, redemption involves the cancelling of a debt the individual cannot pay on his own.

While literal, physical slavery is incomprehensible to us today, we nevertheless live much like slaves in our relationship to sin. On our own, we cannot escape from its consequence: death. We need a redeemer, someone to pay the debt that then gives us the forgiveness from sin we cannot give ourselves.

We have such a redeemer. He is Jesus Christ, who paid our debt not with money, but with his own blood.

It's definitely relief. It's like an epiphany.
— Fifth-year lacrosse senior Sam Payton on the national title

To accept Jesus Christ as your savior is to believe his death was a selfless act of redemption.

RUN FOR IT

Read John 20:1-10.

"Peter and the other disciple started for the tomb. Both were running, but the other disciple outran Peter and reached the tomb first" (vv. 3-4).

Harold Bradley, Duke's "mild-mannered 'gentleman coach,'" had to win over a team that he inherited. He did it by letting them run.

Bradley took over Duke's basketball program in 1950 under extremely difficult circumstances. Cancer forced popular and successful coach Gerry Gerard to leave the team shortly before the 1950-51 season started. That's when Bradley came in. (See Devotion No. 30.)

He arrived in Durham in November with the season upon him and with players he knew nothing about and who didn't know much about him. His first practice didn't impress the players too much; all they did was run to the free-throw line and shoot. Team star Dick Groat said he didn't know what to think. "We had never heard of him," Bernie Janicki said. "We had no idea who he was." Janicki was the team MVP in 1954 as a senior and still holds the school record with 31 rebounds in a game and 476 boards in a season.

But Bradley introduced a style of play that won the players over totally -- after they got over the initial shock. "He told us he wanted the ball on the glass 100 times a game," Janicki said. "We looked at him like he was crazy." In other words, Bradley wanted to run and then run some more. He pointed out to his players that making one-third of 100 shots was better than making half of 50 shots. "After that we loved him," Janicki said.

So the Blue Devils ran. "The fast break was our offense," Janicki said. Before Bradley arrived, Duke had never scored 100 points in a game. During Bradley's nine-year tenure, the Blue Devils broke the century mark a dozen times. Running all the way, his 1955 team averaged a school-record 85.2 points per game in an age long before the shot clock and the three-point shot.

Hit the ground running — every morning that's what you do as you leave the house and re-enter the rat race. You run errands; you give someone a run for his money; you always want to be in the running and never run-of-the-mill.

You're always running toward something, such as your goals, or away from something, such as your past. Many of us spend much of our lives attempting to run away from God, the purposes he has for us, and the blessings he is waiting to give us.

No matter how hard or how far you run, though, you can never outrun yourself or God. God keeps pace with you, calling you in the short run to take care of the long run by falling to your knees and running for your life — to Jesus — just as Peter and the other disciple ran that first Easter morning.

On your knees, you run all the way to glory.

We just ran and ran. We wanted to catch the other team with their pants down.
— Rudy D'Emilio, first-team All-ACC 1954, on Bradley's offense

You can run to eternity by going to your knees.

THE ANSWER

Read Colossians 2:2-10.

*"My purpose is that they . . . may know the mystery of
God, namely, Christ, in whom are hidden all the treasures
of wisdom and knowledge" (vv. 2, 3).*

Too many questions. That's why Duke couldn't win a national
championship in 2010. All the answers. That's why they did.

Yes, the pundits said Duke was pretty good, good enough, in
fact, to win the ACC. After all, they returned Jon Scheyer, Kyle
Singler, and Nolan Smith, scorers all. More than the ACC title,
though, was out of the question because of the questions.

To begin with, there was the problem of moving Singler to the
wing from the post. Then there wasn't enough depth in the back-
court. Also, the team didn't really have a go-to guy. But Coach
Mike Krzyzewski came up with some answers, and the players
made them work. The proof lay in the final game.

First question: Singler on the wing. Answer: Singler scored 19
points and was the Final Four MVP. Obviously, the move didn't
turn out to be a problem.

Second question: depth. Answer: Singler, Scheyer and Smith
played 117 out of a possible 120 minutes in the title game, scoring
47 points among them. Obviously, depth wasn't a problem.

Third question: no go-to guy. Answer: At crunch time, when
Butler attempted a jump shot to take the lead with only seven
seconds left, Singler and Brian Zoubek showed they were go-to

guys. The two combined to force the Bulldog to change his shot, which clanged out. Duke had a 61-59 win.

With all the answers for all the questions, the Duke Blue Devils became the answer to another question: Who are the 2010 national champions?

Experience is essentially the uncovering of answers to some of life's questions, both trivial and profound. You often discover to your dismay that as soon as you learn a few answers, the questions change. Your children get older, your health worsens, your financial situation changes, one of Duke's teams struggles unexpectedly — all situations requiring answers to a new set of difficulties.

No answers, though, are more important than those you seek in your search for God and the meaning of life because they will determine your fate for all eternity. Since a life of faith is a journey and not a destination, the meaningful questions you have about life do indeed change both with your circumstances and the relentless march of the years. The "why" or the "what" you ask God when you're a teenager is vastly different from the quandaries you ponder as an adult.

No matter how you phrase the question, though, the answer inevitably centers on Jesus. And that answer never changes.

When you're a driver and you're struggling in the car, you're looking for God to come out of the sky and give you a magical answer.
— NASCAR's Rusty Wallace

It doesn't matter what the question is;
if it has to do with life, temporal or eternal,
the answer lies in Jesus.

BELIEVE IT

Read John 3:16-21.

"For God so loved the world that He gave His only begotten Son, that whoever believes in Him should not perish but have everlasting life" (v. 16 NKJV).

I t's unbelievable." ""It hasn't sunk in yet, but it's unbelievable." So spoke a pair of Duke seniors. But they had better believe it: The Duke women's tennis team had just defeated California to win the 2009 national championship.

It seems that nobody could believe what the Duke women had just done. Those two seniors, Melissa Mang and Jessi Robinson, who both won their singles matches, each spoke of the victory as "unbelievable." Even their head coach, Jamie Ashworth, spoke of the team as "unbelievably resilient."

But it's a fact. On May 19, 2009, the Duke women swept eighth-seeded California 4-0 to claim the program's first and the school's tenth national title. The victory seemed so unbelievable to the women who pulled it off that the player who clinched the championship didn't even know she had done it. Mang hit a forehand winner for what she knew ended her match. But it did more than that: It ended the whole shebang. "I was surprised when everyone came running up to me," Mang said.

Some may have found the Blue-Devil triumph unbelievable, but it was certainly no fluke. In posting a 29-3 record, the women closed the season with 18 straight wins. The third-seeded Blue

Devils whipped No. 2 Georgia 5-2 in the semis and No. 6 Miami 4-1 in the quarters. Winning the NCAA Tournament was actually easier for Duke than claiming the ACC title. In one of the most thrilling matches in tournament history, Duke sophomore Reka Zsilinszka, who would be the MVP of the NCAA tournament, recovered from a triple-match point to win her singles match and clinch the team's 4-3 win and the league championship.

Such a comeback was unbelievable. So was the national title.

What we believe underscores everything about our lives. Our politics. How we raise our children. How we treat other people. Whether we respect others, their property and their lives.

Often, competing belief systems clamor for our attention; we all know persons — maybe friends and family members — who have lost Christianity in all the shuffle and the hubbub.

We turn aside from believing in Christ at our peril, however, because the heart and soul, the very essence of Christianity, is belief. That is, believing that Jesus is the very Son of God and that it is through him – and only through him – that we can find forgiveness and salvation that will reserve a place for us with God.

But believing is more than simply acknowledging intellectually that Jesus is God. Even the demons who serve Satan know that. It is belief so deep that we entrust our lives and our eternity to Christ. We live like we believe it — because we do.

It's unbelievable. I don't even have any words to describe the feeling.
— Jessi Robinson on Duke's national championship

Believe it: Jesus is the way – and the only way
– to eternal life with God.

DOWN AND DIRTY

Read Isaiah 1:15-20.

"Though your sins are like scarlet, they shall be as white as snow; though they are red as crimson, they shall be like wool" (v. 18).

When Bill Werber came to Duke University in 1926, he expected to find a calm, beautiful campus. What he found instead was such a dirty, noisy mess that it almost drove him off.

In 1930, Werber was Duke's first basketball All-America. Eddie Cameron always insisted that Werber was the finest player he ever recruited. What made Werber special, Cameron said, was that he drove for the basket relentlessly and "could jump and get a shot off in the air." That doesn't sound too special until we realize that Werber played in an era when almost every shot was a set shot with both the player's feet planted on the floor.

Werber arrived at Duke in the fall of 1926 from Washington, D.C., "expecting to find a tranquil green oasis, magnolia trees and ivy walls." What he found was one big, ugly mess.

When Werber showed up, the university was in the throes of the rather sloppy transformation from Trinity College to Duke University. A railroad track ran right into the quad and disgorged a cargo of bricks every night, covering everything in the area with dust. Woe be to the unwitting person who went for a walk on a rainy day: "His clothes splattered and wet, he suffered further misery by becoming mired in mud."

BLUE DEVILS

In the dorms, the doors lacked hardware so when a breeze ran through the floors, according to Werber, "those doors would bang, bang down one side of the corridor and up the other, never in unison. Sometimes this clatter would last all night long."

The workers would start at daylight. "All of this, plus the heat, dust, noise and confusion, was just too much," Werber said. "I almost decided to pack up and go home." Fortunately for Duke history, though, he stayed, and led the school's basketball surge.

Maybe you've never slopped any pigs; you may not be a fan of mud boggin'. Still, you've worked on your car, planted a garden, played touch football in the rain, or endured some military training. You've been dirty.

Dirt, grime, and mud aren't the only sources of stains, however. We can also get dirty spiritually by not living in accordance with God's commands, by doing what's wrong, or by not doing what's right. We all experience temporary shortcomings and failures; we all slip and fall into the mud.

Whether we stay there or not, though, is a function of our relationship with Jesus. For the followers of Jesus, sin is not a way of life; it's an abnormality, so we don't stay in the filth. We seek a spiritual bath by expressing regret and asking for God's pardon in Jesus' name. God responds by washing our soul white as snow with his forgiveness.

Duke in September, 1926, was a sorry-looking place.

— *Bill Werber*

**When your soul gets dirty,
a powerful and thorough cleansing agent
is available for the asking: God's forgiveness.**

PLAN AHEAD

Read Psalm 33:1-15.

"The plans of the Lord stand firm forever, the purposes of his heart through all generations" (v. 11).

I t went just like we planned." So declared Coach Mike Krzyzewski after a win over UCLA's Bruins sent Duke into the 1990 NCAA regional finals. Unfortunately, he was joking; not very much in the topsy-turvy 1989-90 season went according to plan.

Seniors Alaa Abdelnaby, Phil Henderson, and Robert Brickey, junior Greg Koubek, and sophomore Christian Laettner gave the Devils a wealth of experience. But after a 12-2 start, Brickey went down with a knee injury. When he returned, "he never regained the scoring form he had displayed before getting hurt."

Even some of the games didn't follow anybody's plan. Against Maryland, with two seconds left, freshman point guard Bobby Hurley made two free throws for a 95-93 lead. In those seemingly endless two seconds, Maryland got the ball down court, Brickey blocked a shot, and a Terrapin player picked the ball up and shot. The Devils were so sure the shot came after the buzzer that they emptied onto the floor in celebration. The refs said it was good, though, sending the game into overtime. Duke finally won 114-111. "There is no explanation," Coach K said.

The team lost in the ACC semifinals, prompting a locker-room tirade from Henderson, who said the team had "a bunch of babies" and "too many quitters." His words apparently hit home because

BLUE DEVILS

Duke didn't lose again until the national championship game.

About that regional semifinal that didn't go according to the best laid plans. UCLA wiped out a nine-point Devil lead early in the last half, and then Abdelnaby and Laettner collected their fourth fouls within ten seconds of each other. So Henderson took over, scoring 13 straight points. Duke won 90-81.

And Coach K's tongue-in-cheek plan? "We wanted to get everyone in foul trouble and then pray Phil would save us."

Successful living takes planning. You go to school to improve your chances for a better paying job. You use blueprints to build your home. You plan your investments with an eye toward retirement. You map out your vacation to have the best time. You even plan your children — sometimes.

Your best-laid plans, however, sometimes get wrecked by events and circumstances beyond your control. The economy goes into the tank; a debilitating illness strikes; a hurricane hits. Life is capricious and thus no plans — not even your best ones — are foolproof.

But you don't have to go it alone. God has plans for your life that guarantee success as God defines it if you will make him your planning partner. God's plan for your life includes joy, love, peace, kindness, gentleness, and faithfulness, all the elements necessary for truly successful living for today and for all eternity. And God's plan will not fail.

If you don't know where you're going, you will wind up somewhere else.
— Yogi Berra

Your plans may ensure a successful life;
God's plans will ensure a successful eternity.

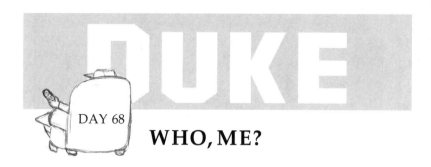

WHO, ME?

Read Judges 6:11-23.

"'But Lord,' Gideon asked, 'how can I save Israel? My clan is the weakest in Manasseh, and I am the least in my family'" (v. 15).

Kevin Thompson had his life in order. That order included graduation, marriage, and work. It did not include football — and then he got a phone call.

In the spring of 1999, Thompson was about to graduate from Duke in May. After his marriage, Elizabeth and he would begin their work in campus ministries for the Greater Atlanta Church of Christ. In his previous three seasons, Thompson had played sparingly at quarterback. He had completed 21 of 59 passes for 288 yards and was ready to move on with his life.

But then came the surprise phone call from Blue Devil football coach Carl Franks. He asked Thompson to consider returning to the team for his final year of eligibility.

Thompson had been so sure of his decision that he hadn't even participated in spring football. "It was three or four weeks before the wedding" when Franks called, Thompson said. He talked to a number of people and prayed about it. His church leaders told him to go for it, so Thompson made his decision: "I told Coach Franks I would come back if I had an equal opportunity to start."

Spencer Romine emerged as the starter for the season opener, but he suffered a separated shoulder in the game. The following week against Northwestern, Thompson came off the bench to complete 12 passes for 153 yards, and on Monday, Franks named him the starter for the Vanderbilt game.

"It's definitely exciting, something I've always wanted to do," Thompson said. He was ready. Said Duke quarterbacks coach Ben Bennett, "Once he decided to come back, he has really immersed himself in football." Much to Kevin Thompson's surprise.

Sometimes the surprises you've experienced in life haven't been as pleasant as Kevin Thompson's was. You know, the ones that bring with them a sinking "who, me?" feeling. How about that time the teacher called on you when you hadn't done a lick of homework? Or the night the hypnotist pulled you out of a room full of folks to be his guinea pig? You've had the wide-eyed look and the turmoil in your midsection when you were suddenly singled out and found yourself in a situation you neither sought nor were prepared for.

You may feel the same way Gideon did about being called to serve God in some way. You quail at the very notion of being audacious enough to teach Sunday school, lead a small group study in your home, serve on your church's governing body, or coordinate a high school prayer club. After all, who in the world is worthy enough to do things like that?

The truth is that nobody is — but that doesn't seem to matter to God. And it's his opinion, not yours, that counts.

I was through with football.
— *Kevin Thompson in the spring of 1999*

**You're right in that no one is worthy to serve God,
but the problem is that doesn't matter to God.**

THE SUB

Read Galatians 3:10-14.

"Christ redeemed us from the curse of the law by becoming a curse for us" (v. 13).

The team's Most Valuable Player fouled out with 3:54 left to play against UNC. So on came a little-used sub who sparked the Blue Devils to a win in one of the rivalry's greatest games ever.

Mike Lewis was second-team All-America and first-team All-ACC in 1968. His specialty was rebounding; he led the league in rebounding in both '66 and '68 and set the Duke record for best career rebounding average (broken by Randy Denton).

Lewis was from Missoula, Montana, and getting there from Durham presented some challenges for the Duke coaches. After changing planes several times and enduring a stormy flight, Duke assistant Bucky Waters, more than a tad green and unsteady on his feet, greeted Lewis by saying, "You better be good."

He was, right on through his final home game on March 2, 1968. Lewis scored 18 points and hauled down 18 boards as the 10th-ranked Blue Devils battled the No. 3 Heels. He fouled out, though, with 3:54 left and Duke behind by three. Junior Fred Lind took his place. He had played little, scoring only twelve points the entire season. "It was agonizing watching from the bench," Lewis said. "I felt like I was letting my team down."

But Lind responded with the game of his life. He made two free throws that sent the game into overtime and a jump shot that

BLUE DEVILS

sent the game into a second overtime. Duke eventually won 87-86 in three extra periods.

And Lewis' agitation on the bench? As he watched fretfully, Lewis said afterwards, "It occurred to me that I couldn't possibly do any better than Freddie was doing. So I sat back and tried to enjoy it." Lind finished the night with 16 points, nine rebounds, and three blocks. "It was almost surreal," said senior forward Joe Kennedy of the substitute's performance.

Wouldn't it be cool if you had a substitute like Fred Lind for all life's hard stuff? Telling of a death in the family? Call in your sub. Breaking up with your boyfriend? Job interview? Chemistry test? Crucial presentation at work? Let the sub handle it.

We do have such a substitute, but not for the trivial or profound matters of life. Instead, Jesus is our substitute for matters of life and death. Since Jesus has already stepped up and made it for us, we don't have to make the sacrifice God demands for forgiveness and salvation.

One of the ironies of our age is that many people desperately grope for a substitute for Jesus. Mysticism, human philosophies such as Scientology, false religions such as Hinduism and Islam, cults, New Age approaches that preach self-fulfillment without responsibility or accountability – they and others like them are all pitiful, inadequate substitutes for Jesus.

Accept no substitutes. It's Jesus or nothing.

Like all reserves, I was sure I could play if I just had the chance.
— Fred Lind on his great performance against UNC

**There is no substitute for Jesus,
the consummate substitute.**

THE SUB   139

THE FAME GAME

Read 1 Kings 10:1-10, 18-29.

"King Solomon was greater in riches and wisdom than all the other kings of the earth. The whole world sought audience with Solomon" (vv. 23-24).

The 1991-92 team members were so famous and drew so many groupies that they once had to sneak out a back window to get to the team bus. And it was an out-of-town ACC game!

Grant Hill, Brian Davis, Christian Laettner, Bobby Hurley, and Thomas Hill were the famous faces of the 1991-92 Blue Devils that started the season No. 1 and finished it that way with a 71-51 defeat of Michigan in the NCAA finals. On Jan. 8, those famous faces and their teammates beat Maryland 83-66 in College Park.

At Cole Field House, the teams exited the locker rooms from a common runway. From Capitol Heights, MD, Davis dressed after the game intending to go visit with family members and friends. "Brian, there's no way, man," one of the managers yelled at him. Davis stuck his head out of the locker room door and understood what the manager meant.

"I couldn't get to my family," Davis said. "It was incredible. I've never seen a mob like that, screaming and yelling, and just trying to get a piece of you." Hundreds of fans had jammed the exit ramp wanting to mix with the Blue Devils or get an autograph. The players waited a while, but so did the crowd. Finally, the players climbed out a back window and scampered to the team bus.

BLUE DEVILS

It didn't help much. A large crowd of fans had already located the Duke bus and was waiting there to ambush the players. "I've never seen anything like what happened," said Davis. "Watching this outpouring of adoration from Duke groupies of all ages" were the dejected Maryland players. Even on the road, Duke was famous.

Have you ever wanted to be famous? Hanging out with other rich and famous people, having folks with microphones listen to what you say, throwing money around like toilet paper, meeting adoring and clamoring fans, signing autographs, and posing for the paparazzi before you climb into your imported sports car?

Many of us yearn to be famous, well-known in the places and by the people that we believe matter. That's all fame amounts to: strangers knowing your name and your face.

The truth is that you are already famous where it really does matter, which excludes TV's talking heads, screaming teenagers, moviegoers, or Washington, D.C., power brokers. You are famous because Almighty God knows your name, your face, and everything about you.

If a persistent photographer snapped you pondering this fame — the only kind that has eternal significance — would the picture show the world unbridled joy or the shell-shocked expression of a mug shot?

No wonder they hate us.
— Mickie Krzyzewski on seeing the mob and Maryland's players

**You're already famous because God knows
your name and your face, which may be either
reassuring or terrifying.**

AMAZING!

Read: Luke 4:31-36.

"All the people were amazed and said to each other, 'What is this teaching? With authority and power he gives orders to evil spirits and they come out!'" (v. 36)

What can you do after your coach says you don't have a chance? If you're the Blue Devils, you go out and pull off one of the most amazing victories in the history of Duke football.

Only head coach Steve Spurrier knew whether he was engaging in brilliant psychological warfare or simply being brutally honest when he told his team they had only one chance in a million of beating 7th-ranked Clemson on Sept. 30, 1989. Spurrier instructed his team just to stay loose and have fun instead of worrying about pulling off the improbable upset.

The first half certainly didn't give any indications of an upset so monumental it would spur the Devils to the league championship. The Tigers roared out to a 14-0 lead. In the last half, though, Duke blew Clemson away to take an amazing 21-17 win.

Quarterback Billy Ray hit fullback Chris Brown with a 7-yard touchdown pass with 3:18 left to play that was the game winner. The score capped a 73-yard drive.

Clemson still had one last chance to save itself. Led by tackles from linebacker George Edwards and end Preston Anderson, though, the Duke defense made one last magnificent stand and preserved the upset. For the half, Clemson managed only 46 yards rushing and 95 yards of total offense.

"Hardly anybody gave us a chance," Spurrier conceded. "They thought we couldn't stop anybody and we'd just go out and throw it around a little." Added the old ball coach about the amazing win, "We'll all remember this one the rest of our lives."

The word *amazing* defines the limits of what you believe to be plausible or usual. The Grand Canyon, the birth of your children, a Duke win late in the game – they're amazing! You've never seen anything like that before!

Some people in Galilee felt the same way when they encountered Jesus. Jesus amazed them with the authority of his teaching and his ability to heal even those with the worst afflictions. He also wowed them with his power over spirit beings. People everywhere just couldn't quit talking about him.

It would have been amazing had they not been amazed. They were, after all, witnesses to the most amazing spectacle in the history of the world: God himself was right there among them walking, talking, teaching, preaching, and healing.

Their amazement should be a part of your life too because Jesus still lives. The almighty and omnipotent God of the universe seeks to spend time with you every day — because he loves you. Amazing!

It's amazing. Some of the greatest characteristics of being a winning football player are the same ones it's true of to be a Christian man.
— Bobby Bowden

Everything about God is amazing,
but perhaps most amazing of all is that
he loves us and desires our company.

RAIN CHECK

Read Genesis 9:8-17.

*"I establish my covenant with you: Never again will all
life be cut off by the waters of a flood; never again will
there be a flood to destroy the earth" (v. 11).*

Duke's football coach was so intent on his team working hard
for the bowl game that he found a place where rain wasn't in the
forecast and took them there to practice.

The Blue Devils of 1960 ended the season at 7-3 and on a down
note with successive losses to North Carolina and UCLA. Nevertheless, they received a bid to the Cotton Bowl to take on heavily
favored Arkansas. Coach Bill Murray decided his team needed to
seriously rededicate itself to football. "Coach Murray said we had
to regroup," recalled Art Gregory, a two-time All-ACC tackle and
twice winner of the Jacobs Blocking Trophy as the league's best
blocker. That meant lots of practice of the two-a-day kind. "It was
just like preseason," Gregory remembered. "We were on campus
after everyone else had gone."

Murray went so far as to dig up some research that showed
which place in Texas had the least chance of rain that time of
the year. It was San Antonio, not Dallas, the home of the Cotton
Bowl. So the Blue Devils left Christmas Day for San Antonio and
some more two-a-day practices. The team bivouacked in a high
school, which according to Gregory was "a drab place, with leaky
showers. The field had dirt mounds all over it." Later on, Murray

moved the team to "a hotel occupied by elderly retirees, who would have tea at 5 o'clock. There were no distractions." Even when the Devils finally arrived in Dallas, they continued to work, leaving a players banquet early one day so they could practice.

It wasn't much fun, but all that work worked. With only 2:45 left, quarterback Don Altman threw a touchdown pass to end Tee Moorman, and Art Browning kicked the extra point for the 7-6 upset. It didn't rain that day in Dallas either.

The kids are on go for their picnic. Your golf game is set. You have rib eyes and smoked sausage ready for the grill when the gang comes over tonight. And then it rains.

Sometimes you can slog on through a downpour as football teams usually do. Often, however, the rain simply washes away your carefully laid plans, and you can't do anything about it except maybe throw your hands up and retreat indoors.

Rain falls when and where it wants to without checking with you. It answers only to God, the one who controls the heavens from which it comes, the ground on which it falls, and everything in between — territory that should include you.

Interestingly enough, this God who has absolute dominance over the rain will take control of your life only if you let him. In daily seeking his will for your life, you discover that you can live so as to be walking in the sunshine even when it's raining.

Don't pray when it rains if you don't pray when the sun shines.
— Pitcher and philosopher Leroy "Satchel" Paige

Into each life some rain must fall,
but you can live in the glorious light
of God's love even during a downpour.

WINNER'S CIRCLE

Read 1 John 5:1-12.

"Who is it that overcomes the world? Only he who believes that Jesus is the Son of God" (v. 5).

The Blue Devils' 75-61 win over Wake Forest on Jan. 22, 2000, was just another defeat of a conference opponent by a program that wins as few ever have. This particular win was special, however; it marked for all time that nobody has ever won in the ACC as Duke has.

"We stand alone," said senior Chris Carrawell after the win. He was exactly right. The win was the Devils' 28th straight ACC regular-season conference victory, which broke the old record of 27 straight set by N.C. State from 1972-75. Carrawell said he couldn't even recall the last time Duke had lost a conference game during the regular season. For the record, it was on Feb. 5, 1998, to North Carolina.

Exactly aware of the situation and circumstances – as always – a small contingent of Cameron Crazies made the trip and chanted "28 straight! 28 straight!" as the clock wound down. They saw freshman point guard Jason Williams put up 19 points and the Duke defense hold the Deacons to 33.8 percent shooting.

Coach Mike Krzyzewski called the record win streak a "terrific thing," but said he never used it as motivation or a goal on which the team was to focus. Wake Forest coach Dave Odom said the streak was "quite an achievement. In this league, to do what their coaching staff has done and the way their players have handled it [is] truly remarkable."

The streak began on Feb. 8, 1998, with a 65-49 win over N.C. State. The Blue Devils won four games before the regular season ended and were 16-0 in the conference in 1998-99. They won three more league games after the win over Wake to up the record to 31 straight. A loss to Maryland on Feb. 9 ended the run, which was just more evidence of what the Blue Devils do best: win.

Like athletic events, life itself is a competition. You vie against all the other job or college applicants. You compete against others for a date. You try to outdo your peers in the office. Sibling rivalry is real; just ask your brother or sister.

Inherent in any competition or any situation in which you try hard to win is the involvement of an antagonist. You always have an opponent to overcome, even if it's an inanimate video game, a golf course, or even yourself.

Nobody wants to be numbered among life's losers. We recognize them when we see them, and maybe mutter a prayer that says something like, "There but for the grace of God go I."

But one adversary will defeat us: Death will claim us all. We can turn the tables on this foe, though; we can defeat the grave. A victory is possible, however, only through faith in Jesus Christ. With Jesus, we have hope beyond death because we have life.

With Jesus, we win. For all of eternity.

We want to keep it going.
— *Chris Carrawell on the Duke conference win streak*

Death is the ultimate opponent;
Jesus is the ultimate victor.

PRESSURE COOKER

Read 1 Kings 18:16-40.

"Answer me, O Lord, answer me, so these people will know that you, O Lord, are God" (v. 37).

Even his teammates made it clear: The pressure was on Billy King in the biggest game of his career. So he responded to the pressure by scoring three points. You might say he didn't take the pressure well; you would be wrong.

King was a scorer in high school, but it was his defensive talents that got him playing time his freshman and sophomore seasons at Duke. He gradually came to relish his role as the team's defensive stopper. He moved into the starting lineup as a junior in 1986-87 and took over the "primary ball-pressure role" as a senior. "The whole basis of Coach K's defense was ball pressure," King recalled. "I was like the middle linebacker. I made it a point to make sure everybody was in the right position."

King ran into his toughest and most pressure-packed challenge in the 1988 NCAA regional finals. The top-ranked Temple Owls had only one scary offensive weapon: guard Mark Macon, the national freshman of the year who had averaged more than 20 points a game. "Okay, Billy, you've got to stop this guy" was the word King got from the teammates who hung out in his room the night before the game. Everyone knew Duke's chances "very much depended on King's ability to control Macon."

As he always did, King prepared by watching a lot of film. His first impression was "This guy is real good." But as he studied, he found a weakness: Macon never liked to go right. So if he could force the freshman to go to his right, King could shut him down.

He did just that, holding Macon to 13 points on six-of-29 shooting. Macon missed seven of his eight three-point tries and never went to the foul line. Duke won 63-53. When the buzzer sounded, Billy King finally let the pressure go. He was so overcome with emotion, he broke down and cried.

You live every day with pressure. As Elijah did so long ago and as Billy King did against Temple, you lay it on the line with everybody watching. Your family, coworkers, or employees — they all depend on you. You know the pressure of a job evaluation, of a deadline, of taking the risk of asking someone to go out with you, of driving in rush-hour traffic.

Help in dealing with daily pressure is readily available, and the only price you pay for it is your willingness to believe. God will give you the grace to persevere if you ask prayerfully.

And while you may need some convincing, the pressures of daily living are really small potatoes since they all will pass. The real pressure comes when you stare into the face of eternity because what you do with it is irrevocable and forever. You can handle that pressure easily enough by deciding for Jesus. Eternity is then taken care of; the pressure's off – forever.

I never thought that I would be a defensive guy.
— Billy King on his specialty with the Blue Devils

The greatest pressure you face in life
concerns where you will spend eternity,
which can be dealt with by deciding for Jesus.

SWEET WORDS

Read John 8:1-11.

"'Then neither do I condemn you,' Jesus declared. 'Go now and leave your life of sin'" (v. 11).

While it sounds ludicrous today, there was a time when Mike Krzyzewski needed someone to tell him that he was a good coach. Athletic director Tom Butters did exactly that in a unique way.

When Butters hired Krzyzewski in 1980, he made sure his new coach knew everything wasn't peaches and cream in Durham. He said "we would have one decent year, then we'd go through rebuilding," Krzyzewski recalled. Butters "painted a rougher picture than what I thought it would be."

Not that Duke didn't have some players. Kenny Dennard, Gene Banks, and Vince Taylor all came back from a team that had gone to the NCAA Tournament. So, exactly as Butters had said, Duke had a decent year in 1980-81, winning 17 games and playing in the NIT. Unfortunately, Butters was right, too, about the rebuilding years. The next two seasons Duke went 21-34 and a disastrous 7-21 in the ACC. With a couple of recruiting classes on hand, the 1983-84 team won 14 of its first 15 games, but then lost four straight ACC contests. People started howling again.

That's when Butters called his beleaguered coach into his office. He told Krzyzewski, "We've got a public who doesn't know how good you are. We've got press who are too stupid to tell them how good you are. And the biggest problem right now is I'm not sure you know how good you are." With that pronouncement, Butters tossed a new five-year contract across the desk.

When he realized what the document was, Krzyzewski teared up. Then he said, "Tom, you don't need to do this." Butters replied, "I not only have to do it. I need to do it right now."

Thus affirmed, Krzyzewski proceeded to become a legend.

You make a key decision. All excited, you tell your best friend or spouse and then anxiously wait for a reaction. "Boy, that was dumb" is the answer you get.

Maybe a friend's life is spiraling out of control into disaster. Alcohol, affairs, drugs, unemployment. Do you pretend you don't know that messed-up person?

Everybody needs affirmation in some degree. That is, we all occasionally need someone to say something positive about us, that we are worth something, and that God loves us. Tom Butters did just that for Mike Krzyzewski and looked what happened.

The follower of Jesus does what our Lord did when he encountered someone whose life was a shambles. Rather than seeing what they were, he saw what they could become. Life is hard; it breaks us all to some degree. To be like Jesus, we see past the problems of the broken and the hurting and envision their potential, understanding that not condemning them is not the same thing as condoning what they have done.

You tell [everyone] you've been extended five more years and let's let the people know.
— *Tom Butters to Coach K on announcing his contract extension*

**The greatest way to affirm lost persons
is to lead them to Christ.**

CHEAP TRICKS

Read Acts 19:11-20.

"The evil spirit answered them, 'Jesus I know, and I know about Paul, but who are you?'" (v. 15)

The man who "revolutionized the ACC at quarterback" was a part of one of the most famous trick plays in ACC history — and he didn't even touch the ball on the play.

In 1966, Duke coach Tom Harp was recruiting Wes Chesson, who asked about other quarterbacks. Harp replied that they were also recruiting "a lanky guy named Leo Hart. We'll probably move him to wide receiver." "Good," Chesson replied. "I'll need someone to throw to." It didn't turn out that way; instead, Chesson wound up on the receiving end of a bunch of Hart passes.

In 1967, Hart "entered a football world dominated by conservative, three-yards-and-a-cloud-of-dust football." He changed all that, bringing a wide-open passing offense to the staid league. He became eligible for varsity competition in 1968 and immediately grabbed hold of the starting job and never let it go.

In Duke's fourth game, he passed for 249 yards; the following week Hart had the first 300-yard passing game in Duke history. He went on to a fabulous career that put him into the North Carolina Sports Hall of Fame. He became the only quarterback in ACC history to be first-team All-ACC three times.

One of Hart's most famous plays didn't involve a pass at all. In the last game of the 1969 season, Duke and UNC were tied 7-7 in the third quarter. In studying films, Harp had noticed that the Carolina defense turned its back to the ball when they huddled, so the Devils prepared a trick play to take advantage of that.

Hart ran an option and then bent down ostensibly to tie a shoe. With UNC's defense huddled up, end Marcel Courtillet picked up the ball and tossed it to Chesson, who went 53 yards for a touchdown. The trick play spurred Duke to a 17-13 win.

Scam artists are everywhere — and they love trick plays. An e-mail encourages you to send money to some foreign country to get rich. That guy at your front door offers to resurface your driveway at a ridiculously low price. A TV ad promises a pill to help you lose weight without diet or exercise.

You've been around; you check things out before deciding. The same approach is necessary with spiritual matters, too, because false religions and bogus Christian denominations abound. The key is what any group does with Jesus. Is he the son of God, the ruler of the universe, and the only way to salvation? If not, then what the group espouses is something other than the true Word of God.

The good news about Jesus does indeed sound too good to be true, but the only catch is that there is no catch. When it comes to salvation through Jesus Christ, there's no trick lurking in the fine print. There's just the truth, right there for you to see.

We never thought it would work that well. Easiest touchdown I ever had.
> *— Wes Chesson on the trick play against UNC*

God's promises through Jesus sound too good to be true, but the only catch is that there is no catch.

TIME FOR A CHANGE

Read Romans 6:1-14.

"Just as Christ was raised from the dead through the glory of the Father, we too may live a new life" (v. 4).

Basketball Times called Shane Battier "the most sought-after high school player in the country" in 1996. So this successful prep star came to Duke and set about changing his shot.

Battier is a Duke legend. As a senior and the Final Four MVP in 2001, he led the Blue Devils to the national championship. He was both the ACC and the National Player of the Year. For three straight years, he was the national defensive player of the year. He was the first player in ACC history to finish his career with at least 1,500 points, 500 rebounds, 200 assists, 200 steals, and 200 blocks. His number 31 was retired by the Blue Devils.

When he joined the team in the fall of 1997, Battier found his niche as a defensive player, averaging 7.6 points per game. His sophomore numbers were a little better with 9.1 points per game for the 37-2 team that lost to Connecticut in the finals. "I knew we had plenty of great scorers," Battier said about the 1999 team. "Defense was what I did best. That was my role."

That all changed, though, his junior season. He averaged 17.4 points per game, an output that was a prelude to his superb senior season when he averaged 19.9 points per game. Along the way, Battier "established himself as one of the deadliest long-range shooters in college basketball."

BLUE DEVILS

Despite his lowly offensive statistics his first two seasons, Battier was clearly ready when he was called upon to change his game from defense to offense. That was in large part because he set about intentionally changing his shot after his freshman season. "I was a good shooter in high school, but I knew the form on my jump shot would not hold up in college," he said. He worked with former Duke guard and pro instructor Chip Engelland. "It took nine months for that to pay off," Battier said.

But the change paid off big-time: in a national championship.

Anyone who asserts no change is needed in his or her life isn't paying attention. Every life has doubt, worry, fear, failure, frustration, unfulfilled dreams, and unsuccessful relationships in some combination. The memory and consequences of our past often haunt and trouble us.

As important a step as it may be, simply recognizing the need for change in our lives doesn't mean the changes that will bring about hope, joy, peace, and fulfillment will occur. We need some power greater than ourselves, or we wouldn't be where we are.

So where can we turn to? Where lies the hope for a changed life? It lies in an encounter with him who is the Lord of all Hope: Jesus Christ. For a life turned over to Jesus, change is inevitable. With Jesus in charge, the old self with its painful and destructive ways of thinking, feeling, loving, and living is transformed.

A changed life is always only a talk with Jesus away.

[Chip Engelland] helped me develop a way to change my shot.
— Shane Battier

**In Jesus lie the hope and the power
that change lives.**

DREAM WORLD

Read Joel 2:26-28.

"Your old men will dream dreams, your young men will see visions" (v. 28).

Notions of championships — league, tournament, and national — were little but rather far-fetched dreams when the 2009-10 Duke basketball season began. Just call the team the Dreamcatchers.

The Blue Devils had not been to a Final Four since the 2003-04 season. They had not won a national championship since 2001, a heartbeat for most programs, a drought for Duke. And when the 2009-10 squad got together for the first time, they seemed like an unlikely bunch to make anybody's dreams come true. They needed Nolan Smith to emerge as a go-to scorer. Brian Zoubek and Miles Plumlee had to develop as forces inside. As one writer put it, though, "A funny thing happened. All three delivered."

What also happened was a dream season. Maybe folks started realizing something special was up in the last game of the regular season, a trap game against UNC. The Heels had slid into the nether regions of the ACC, but an upset of Duke could salvage the season. Yeah, right. Duke "attacked, controlled and dominated" and blasted UNC 82-50. The win over North Carolina "was a turning point for us," declared Smith.

The squad kept the dreams alive when they beat Baylor 78-71 in the East Region finals in what was called "arguably the most compelling [game] of the first two weeks of the tournament." After

BLUE DEVILS

the game, senior guard Jon Scheyer said what everybody was really thinking: Advancing to the Final Four "is a dream come true. It just is."

The last of those fanciful dreams of six months before proceeded to come true in Indianapolis with wins over West Virginia and Butler: The Duke Blue Devils were national champions.

You have dreams. Maybe to make a lot of money. Write the great American novel. Or have the fairy-tale romance. But dreams often are crushed beneath the weight of everyday living; reality, not dreams, comes to occupy your time, attention, and effort. You've come to understand that achieving your dreams requires a combination of persistence, timing, and providence.

But what if your dreams don't come true because they're not good enough? That is, they're based on the alluring but totally unreliable promises of the world rather than the true promises of God, which are a sure thing.

All too often we settle for mundane lives, forgetting that God calls us to greatness because his dreams for us are grander than our dreams for ourselves are. Such greatness occurs, though, only when our dreams and God's will for our lives are the same. Your dreams should be worthy of your best — and worthy of God's involvement in making them come true.

An athlete cannot run with money in his pocket. He must run with hope in his heart and dreams in his head.
— Olympic gold medalist Emil Zatopek

**Dreams based on the world's promises
are often crushed; those based
on God's promises are a sure thing.**

IN THE KNOW

Read John 4:19-26, 39-42.

"They said to the woman, . . . 'Now we have heard for ourselves, and we know that this man really is the Savior of the world'" (v. 42).

Coach Harold Bradley practiced his team in a particular way for an upcoming game with Kentucky, just as though he knew something about the game. As it turned out, he must have.

In February 1956, Duke played the 8th-ranked Wildcats down to the wire in Lexington before losing 81-76. As sophomore reserve Hayes Clement, who had played little, made his way to the locker room, he was accosted by a little old lady who was "probably about 75 years old," Clement recalled. "She started hitting me with her umbrella, while screaming, 'You almost beat us! You almost beat us!'" Ducking out of her way, Clement shouted, "Don't take it out on me! I didn't have anything to do with it."

In a return game in Durham on Dec. 18, 1956, odds were that the Wildcats would whip Duke again even without that angry senior citizen and her parasol of mass destruction. The Blue Devils had not beaten Kentucky since 1930 and had never beaten the Wildcats in Durham. As he prepared his team, though, Bradley changed his practices in a way that indicated he had some insight into the game: He gave extra attention to the full-court press.

Early on, it looked as though it wouldn't matter. The Wildcats jumped out to a 30-15 lead and led 53-40 early in the last half. With

14 minutes left, though, Kentucky's playmaking guard fouled out. Bradley immediately switched to the press.

Bobby Joe Harris, Duke's own playmaker, proceeded to grab one steal after another, and the Devils rallied. Harris had three steals in the last two minutes, the latter coming with Duke trailing 84-83 with less than 30 seconds left. Harris passed the ball to Bucky Allen for the game winner in the 85-84 victory, a game that Bradley had prepared his team for as though he knew what was going to happen.

Like Coach Bradley and the Kentucky game, you just know certain things in your life. That your spouse loves you or that you are good at your job, for instance. That tea should be iced and sweetened. That a bad day hunting or fishing is still way better than a good day at work. You know these things even though no mathematician or philosopher can prove any of this on paper.

It's the same way with faith in Jesus. No neat equation or set of logical premises and deductions can prove that Jesus is God's son and the savior of the world. You just know it. You know it in the same way that you know Duke is the only team worth pulling for: with every fiber of your being, with all your heart, your mind, and your soul.

You just know, and because you know him, Jesus knows you. And that is all you really need to know.

It was almost like coach [Harold] Bradley knew what was going to happen. He must have been psychic.
— Duke's Bucky Allen on preparations for the 1956 Kentucky game

A life of faith is lived in certainty and conviction:
You just know you know.

UNEXPECTEDLY

Read Matthew 24:36-51.

"No one knows about that day or hour, not even the angels in heaven, nor the Son, but only the Father" (v. 36).

The Duke women just couldn't get rid of 11th-ranked Vanderbilt until unexpectedly they did it in one trip down the floor: They scored eight points in one possession.

On Dec. 7, 2006, the undefeated and fourth-ranked Blue Devils hosted the undefeated Lady Commodores. The Duke women kept a lead as the last half wore down, but Vanderbilt was still lurking around and dangerous. With less than five minutes to play, Duke's lead was nine.

That's when Duke unexpectedly in the matter of a few seconds ended any hopes the Dores had of a comeback. Duke guard Abby Waner came up with a turnover, hurried downcourt, and passed off to fellow guard Wanisha Smith, who got an easy bucket on a layup. Two points.

The refs whistled an intentional foul on Vanderbilt "for clocking Waner in the face." When the refs allowed Smith's basket, the Vandy coach let them know she was extremely displeased with the call. She repeatedly and vociferously asked for an explanation about the rather strange ruling but all she got for her trouble was a technical foul. (The refs later responded in writing to queries about their decision by referring to the rule book.)

Waner hit one of her two free throws. Three points. Lindsey

BLUE DEVILS

Harding (See Devotion No. 6.) made both of the technical free throws. Five points. Because of the intentional foul, Duke got the ball back. Waner promptly nailed a three-pointer from the right corner to complete an unexpected eight-point swing. Only a moment before the Blue Devils had come down the court leading by nine. Now, with only 4:07 to play, they led by seventeen.

Duke coasted after that to a 69-48 win.

Just like Vanderbilt against Duke, we think we've got a shot at pulling something off in our lives and then the unexpected happens. Quite honestly, about the only thing we can expect from life with any certainty is the unexpected.

God is that way too, suddenly showing up to remind us he's still around. A friend who calls and tells you he's praying for you, a hug from your child or grandchild, a lone lily that blooms in your yard — unexpected moments when the divine comes crashing into our lives with such clarity that it takes our breath away and brings tears to our eyes.

But why shouldn't God do the unexpected? The only factor limiting what God can do in our lives is the paucity of our own faith. We should expect the unexpected from God, this same deity who caught everyone by surprise by unexpectedly coming to live among us as a man, and who will return when we least expect it.

That was a huge play for us. It was still extremely close. I think we really just took the game over from that point.
— Abby Waner on the eight-point play

God continually does the unexpected,
like showing up as Jesus,
who will return unexpectedly.

THE GOOD OLD DAYS

Read Psalm 102.

"My days vanish like smoke; . . . but you remain the same, and your years will never end" (vv. 3, 27).

The good old days." How we miss them and yearn for them. But just maybe, compared to today's game, the good old days of Duke basketball weren't really so good.

For instance, while fans today may criticize refs for calling too many fouls and slowing the game up, in the early days fouls were hardly called at all. H.E. Spence, a substitute on Trinity's first basketball team, remembered that "The only fouls that were certain to be called were when two men ganged up on one, or when a man put both arms around the man he was guarding. Otherwise, he could hold, push and pull all he pleased." With "few fouls called for hacking, tripping, blocking, [or] charging," few shots were even attempted, let alone made.

When Trinity College hosted Wake Forest in early 1906 in the school's first game (See Devotion No. 1.), the goals were true baskets. After a rare successful shot, the ball was pushed out by a broom. Play resumed with a center jump.

Play featured very little dribbling. Players passed the ball the same way they shot it — with two hands. Only one guard could cross the midcourt line to participate in the offense. Each team had a designated free-throw shooter. The Trinity star of that first game was guard "Reddy" White," who led the team with all of four points in the 24-10 loss.

Eligibility rules were quite loose. One of the Trinity starters was Garland Greever, a graduate student. One of the other team members, B.S. Womble, was in law school. The referee for the first game was the head coach of Wake Forest, Trinity's opponent.

While the game itself may not have been aesthetically pleasing, what would become Duke basketball was a success at the gate from the get-go. An overflow crowd packed the gym for that first-ever game back there in those perhaps-not-so-good old days.

It's a brutal truth that time just never stands still. The current of your life sweeps you along until you realize one day you've lived long enough to have a past. Part of it you cling to fondly. The stunts you pulled with your high-school buddies. Your first apartment. That dance with your first love. That special vacation. Those "good old days."

You hold on relentlessly to the memory of those old, familiar ways because of the stability they provide in our uncertain world. They will always be there even as times change and you age.

Another constant exists in your life too. God has been a part of every event in your life that created a memory because he was there. He's always there with you; the question is whether you ignore him or make him a part of your day.

A "good old day" is any day shared with God.

Years ago, you used to fight and run around and chase each other with a jackhammer and stuff like that. Those were the good old days.
— *Dale Earnhardt Jr., on NASCAR track etiquette*

**Today is one of the "good old days"
if you share it with God.**

THE GOOD OLD DAYS   163

THE JESUS WAY

Read Romans 13:8-14.

"The night is nearly over; the day is almost here. So let us put aside the deeds of darkness and put on the armor of light" (v. 12).

On a November night in 2005 after basketball practice, all 6' 10" that was Josh McReynolds sat in a four-year old Toyota Corolla, his knees nearly touching his chin. He wasn't just hitching a ride to his dorm; he was learning The Duke Way. McReynolds' chauffeur was senior star J.J. Redick, who, as he deigned to go out of his way to take an unproven freshman home, was simultaneously demonstrating The Duke Way.

That McReynolds had to bum a ride at all was a byproduct of The Duke Way. Not allowing his freshmen to have cars on campus was just one of the means Coach Mike Krzyzewski devised to build ties between the upperclassmen and the new guys. As quaint as it sounds, carpooling apparently achieves the desired result. "That five to ten minutes a day is easy bonding time, and Josh has become one of my best friends," said Redick. At Duke, the only students "who are expressly prevented from rocking a set of wheels are some of its most recognizable athletes."

The Duke Way was actually hatched during Coach K's days as a cadet at West Point. The buddy system that is part of The Duke Way is a direct descendent of the Army's belief that you "take care of somebody other than yourself," explained Krzyzewski.

BLUE DEVILS

There is no manual. The esoterica of The Duke Way isn't "on page 37 of a guidebook we hand everybody: When to floor-slap," said assistant coach Steve Wojciechowski of the team's "trademark rallying gesture." The Duke Way is absorbed through experience. Or repeatedly watching videos of Duke players "taking charges, diving for balls and displaying unbridled emotion."

The new guys have to learn The Duke Way. After all, it is the way of champions.

You have a way of life that defines and describes you. You're a die-hard Duke fan for starters. Maybe you're married with a family. A city guy or a small-town gal. You wear jeans or a suit to work every day. And then there's your faith.

For the Christian, following Jesus more than anything else should define for the world your way of life. It's basically simple in its concept even if it is downright daunting in its execution. You act toward others in a way that would not embarrass you were your day to be broadcast on Fox News. You think about others in a way that would not humiliate you should your thoughts be the plotline for a new CBS sitcom.

You make your actions and thoughts those of love, at all times, in all things, toward all people. It's the Jesus way of life, and it's the way he has declared that his followers should live. It's also the way to life forever with God.

There are three things we teach kids in practice: work hard, think hard and talk.
— *Mike Krzyzewski on The Duke Way*

To live the Jesus way is to act with love at all times, in all things, and toward all people.

SMART MOVE

Read 1 Kings 4:29-34; 11:1-6.

"[Solomon] was wiser than any other man. . . . As Solomon grew old, his wives turned his heart after other gods, and his heart was not fully devoted to the Lord his God" (vv. 4:31, 11:4).

With his team behind and time growing short, Coach Mike Krzyzewski made a decision that sure didn't seem like a smart move at the time.

While Duke fans may look back at the 1990 team's run to the championship game as their rightful due, the team was in deep trouble prior to the tournament. The Blue Devils lost their last three ACC games and then fell out of the national top 10 with a loss to Georgia Tech in the tournament semifinals.

As expected, behind center Alaa Abdelnaby's 22 points, Duke blew past Richmond 81-46 in the NCAA Tournament's opening round. But in the second round, they ran into trouble against St. John's, trailing 61-53 with about nine minutes left to play. That's when the game's most unusual possession occurred; it included Krzyzewski's decision that went against all the percentages.

Senior captain Robert Brickey was fouled, and the offending St. John's player was hit with a technical foul for protesting too vehemently. Brickey was only a 62 percent free-throw shooter, but he hit both ends of the one-and-one. He then "looked over to the bench to see who was going to shoot the rest." But Coach K surprised him. "He pointed to me," Brickey recalled. "I looked around to make sure he wasn't pointing at anyone else, and there was no one around but me."

Not replacing Brickey with a better shooter didn't seem like a smart move — but he sank them both. Abdelnaby scored to complete a six-point possession, and Duke went on to win 76-72.

Remember that time you ran the car into a mailbox when you spilled hot coffee on your lap? Or that cold morning you fell out of the boat? How about the regrettable time you gave your honey a tool box for her birthday?

Formal education notwithstanding, we all make some dumb moves sometime because time spent in a classroom is not an accurate gauge of common sense. Folks impressed with their own smarts often grace us with erudite pronouncements that we intuitively recognize as flawed, unworkable, or simply wrong.

A good example is the observation that great intelligence and scholarship are not compatible with faith in God. That is, the more we know, the less we believe. But any incompatibility occurs only because we begin to trust in our own wisdom rather than the wisdom of God. We forget, as Solomon did, that God is the ultimate source of all our knowledge and wisdom and that even our ability to learn is a gift from God.

Not smart at all.

On paper, it didn't make sense to keep me at the line, but [Coach K] could see that I was comfortable and went with his instinct.
— Robert Brickey on the decision to let him shoot the free throws

Being truly smart means trusting in God's wisdom rather than only in our own knowledge.

THE WALL

Read Philippians 2:1-11.

". . . that at the name of Jesus every knee should bow, . . . and every tongue confess that Jesus Christ is Lord" (vv. 10, 11).

The Blue Devils flinched, but in the end their defense stood tall.

Missed field goals, turnovers, and a "knee-buckling touchdown pass just when the Blue Devils thought they had a firm handle on [the] game." Duke withstood it all when they took on Vanderbilt on Oct. 25, 2008, in Nashville.

Head coach David Cutcliffe saw all the mistakes, but he also saw a team that refused to wilt. "We did a lot of things that could have cost us the game, but it pleases me that it didn't. Their energy in the fourth quarter was, 'We're not going to be denied.'" When it came down to it, the Blue Devils built a wall and refused to let the Commodore offense breach it.

Quarterback Thaddeus Lewis hit receiver Tony Jackson with a 22-yard touchdown pass to send the Devils into the break with a 7-0 lead. Nick Maggio booted a 42-yard field goal with 5:13 left in the third quarter to up the Duke lead to 10-0.

After that, though, the nature of the game changed as Vandy scored on a 79-yard pass with 13:20 left to play and then threatened the 10-7 Blue-Devil lead the rest of the contest. The Commodores managed a short drive before the Duke defense stopped them, forcing a 42-yard field-goal try that went awry with 7:16 left.

BLUE DEVILS

Vanderbilt then went for it on fourth and 6 from its own 19 with 2:53 left. Cornerback Jabari Marshall batted the pass attempt away. The Commodores had one last try at breaching the Duke defensive wall, but sophomore cornerback Chris Rwabukamba, in for the injured Leon Wright, intercepted a last-ditch pass.

"We're always going to go out there thinking it's on us (the defense)," said linebacker Michael Tauiliili. On this day, it was.

We all build walls. Since we live within ourselves as no one else can, we know our own faults, foibles, and failures more intimately than we wish to. We assume that if people knew the real person inside our skin, they wouldn't like us. Thus, we pose. We put up a false front and hide behind a wall that keeps others from seeing who we really are so we'll appear more acceptable and virtuous to the world.

But it's awfully lonely behind that wall; we hesitate to love and be loved because that means surrender, knocking down the wall and becoming vulnerable. Even when it's Jesus trying to break through, we resist.

But how foolish is that? The purpose of the wall in the first place is to keep others from knowing us, and Jesus already knows absolutely everything there is to know about us. And still he loves us, still he accepts us. To love Jesus isn't surrender; it's victory.

Duke played very well on defense. They thwarted everything we tried to do.
— Vanderbilt head coach Bobby Johnson

We build walls so others won't know us,
but Jesus knows us already and loves us still,
so why keep him out?

MYSTERIOUS WAYS

Read Romans 11:25-36.

"O the depth of the riches and wisdom and knowledge of God! How unsearchable are his judgments and how inscrutable his ways!" (v. 33 NRSV)

The Blue Devils once had a mystery on their hands that was solved only in the dead of night.

Tommy Amaker came to Duke in 1983 and was a four-year starter. He was "a classic point guard, concentrating on distributing the ball and playing defense." He was the national defensive player of the year as a senior in 1987 and was inducted into the Duke Sports Hall of Fame in 2001.

When he was a freshman, Amaker's roommate was 7'2" center Marty Nessley. The two were opposites in many ways. Amaker was meticulous and organized. He "was always on time, always had his classes in order, was always prepared," observed teammate Robert Brickey.

Amaker's bedtime was part of his carefully organized routine: 10 p.m. on weeknights, around 11 p.m. on weekends. Nessley, on the other hand, "was more interested in examining college life."

Nessley constantly battled his weight, and the coaches put him on a strict diet -- but it didn't work. "Marty would come to the training table and barely eat a thing, a salad maybe," said Mark Alarie. "But he couldn't drop any weight. Nobody knew why."

Until one night, when a knock on the door sometime after 1

a.m. awoke Amaker. Nessley got up and answered the door, and shortly thereafter Amaker heard what sounded like rustling coming from Nessley's bed. He turned on a light to see Nessley eating a pizza under the covers. Mystery solved.

People of faith understand that the good Lord often works in mysterious ways. This only serves to make God even more tantalizing because human nature loves a good mystery. We relish the challenge of uncovering what somebody else wants to hide. We are intrigued by a perplexing whodunit such as *NCIS*, a rousing round of Clue, or Perry Mason reruns.

Some mysteries are simply beyond our knowing, however. Events in our lives that are in actuality the mysterious ways of God remain so to us because we can't see the divine machinations. We can see only the results, appreciate that God was behind it all, and give him thanks and praise.

God has revealed much about himself, especially through Jesus, but a great deal still remains unknowable. For instance, why does he tolerate the existence of evil? What does he really look like? Why is he so fond of bugs? What was the inspiration for chocolate?

We know for sure, though, that God is love, and so we proceed with life, assured that one day all mysteries will be revealed.

Through sports, a coach can offer a boy a way to sneak up on the mystery of manhood.
— *Writer Pat Conroy*

**God chooses to keep much about himself
shrouded in mystery, but one day
we will see and understand.**

STRANGE BUT TRUE

Read Isaiah 9:2-7.

"The zeal of the Lord Almighty will accomplish this" (v. 7).

With more than a century of basketball behind them, the Duke Blue Devils have run into some rather strange situations and circumstances over the years.

For instance, Duke once had a player who didn't even make the all-conference team named the league's best player. After the 1966 season, ACC sportswriters named Jack Marin and Bob Verga first team All-ACC and guard Steve Vacendak second-team. "How in the world could anybody pick an all-conference team and leave off Steve Vacendak?" wondered Clemson's coach. Others had the same question. After Vacendak led Duke to the tournament title, those same writers who had failed to put him on the first team named him the ACC Player of the Year. Strange but true.

Duke once had a player thrown out of an opponent's dressing room. During the 1950s, the respective locker rooms weren't very far apart, so after Duke beat Kentucky one night, the players could hear Wildcat coach Adolph Rupp throwing a fit. Duke's Bobby Joe Harris went into the Kentucky locker room to visit an old friend, and Rupp ordered him to get out. He "told me emphatically and colorfully that I had no business being there. He didn't have to tell me twice," Harris said. Strange but true.

Duke once won a game with four of its starters suspended. In

BLUE DEVILS

the 1967 season opener against Penn State, only seven Blue Devil players suited up. Coach Vic Bubas had suspended nine players after they had quaffed some adult beverages at a local night spot. Star guard Bob Verga was the only starter left. Former walk-on Stu McKaig and three little-used sophomores, Fred Lind, Steve Vandenberg, and C.B. Claiborne, joined Verga in the lineup. Verga poured in 38 points and Duke won 89-84. Strange but true.

Some things in life are so strange their existence can't really be explained. How else can we account for curling, tofu, the proliferation of tattoos, and the behavior of teenagers? Isn't it strange that today we have more ways to stay in touch with each other yet are losing the intimacy of personal contact?

And how strange is God's plan to save us? Think a minute about what God did. He could have come roaring down, destroying and blasting everyone whose sinfulness offended him, which, of course, is pretty much all of us. Then he could have brushed off his hands, nodded the divine head, and left a scorched planet in his wake. All in a day's work.

Instead, God came up with a totally novel plan: He would save the world by becoming a human being, letting himself be humiliated, tortured, and killed, thus establishing a kingdom of justice and righteousness that will last forever.

It's a strange way to save the world – but it's true

It may sound strange, but many champions are made champions by setbacks.
— *Olympic champion Bob Richards*

**It's strange but true: God allowed himself
to be killed on a cross to save the world.**

DAY 87

REST EASY

Read Hebrews 4:1-11.

"There remains, then, a Sabbath rest for the people of God; for anyone who enters God's rest also rests from his own work, just as God did from his. Let us, therefore, make every effort to enter that rest" (vv. 9-11).

You're out for the whole year." Somebody had finally told Mike Krzyzewski "what he needed to hear, not what he wanted to hear." He had to take a break. It saved his career, perhaps even his life.

In the summer of 1994, physicians treated Krzyzewski for a pulled hamstring until he learned he had a disk problem. By the time he went to a neurosurgeon, the coach had lost so much of the muscle in his left calf that he couldn't stand with his weight on his left leg. Eight days into fall practice, Krzyzewski underwent surgery.

Within ten days, he was back at practice. He lost weight and was exhausted much of the time, but he kept on working. Eventually, though, he could hardly walk, and his wife, Mickie, intervened by scheduling a doctor's appointment. It just happened to coincide with the start of the day's practice.

Following more tests, Krzyzewski got the good news that he didn't have the cancer that had killed his friend Jim Valvano the previous year. But the doctors agreed on the bad news: He was trying to do too much too soon. They told him he had to take two weeks off, but that didn't help because Krzyzewski went right back to work. The doctors protested that "he wasn't trying to get better, he was trying to get back to his job."

Then they lowered the boom on their reluctant and uncooperative patient. He had to take a whole year off to reverse what was happening to his body. Krzyzewski offered to resign, but athletic director Tom Butters refused to consider it. Krzyzewski missed the last nineteen games of the 1994-95 season, but the frustrating and agonizing time off allowed him to recuperate. Both Coach K and Duke basketball have been going full blast ever since.

As part of the natural rhythm of life, rest is important to maintain physical health. Rest has different images, though: a good eight hours in the sack; a Saturday morning that begins in the backyard with the paper and a pot of hot coffee; a vacation in the mountains, where the most strenuous thing you do is change position in the hot tub.

Rest is also part of the rhythm and the health of our spiritual lives. Often we envision the faithful person as always busy, always doing something for God whether it's teaching Sunday school or showing up at church every time the doors open.

But God himself rested from work, and in blessing us with the Sabbath, he calls us into a time of rest. To rest by simply spending time in the presence of God is to receive spiritual revitalization and rejuvenation. Sleep refreshes your body and your mind; God's rest refreshes your soul.

This is your job whenever you're ready to come back.
— AD Tom Butters to Mike Krzyzewski when he offered to resign

God promises you a spiritual rest
that renews and refreshes your soul.

THE SIMPLE LIFE

Read 1 John 1:5-10.

"If we confess our sins, he is faithful and just and will forgive us our sins and purify us from all unrighteousness" (v. 9).

Amanda Blumenherst has a very simple approach to account for her success on the golf course: "I just hit the ball."

Blumenherst is one of the greatest golfers in Duke and NCAA history. She was three times the ACC Player of the Year and was the league's Co-Player of the Year as a senior in 2009. She is the only golfer in history to be named the National Player of the Year three times. Blumenherst was a three-time All-America who graduated from Duke *magna cum laude* in 2009 and was a key component of the 2006 and 2007 national champions. She won the U.S. Women's Amateur title in 2008 and turned pro in May 2009.

Blumenherst always wanted to be a golfer. In the second grade, she dressed up as a pro golfer complete with polo shirt, shorts, a sweater tied around her neck, a visor and a bag full of clubs. "I'm probably one of the [few who have] stuck with what they dressed up as in second grade" she said.

But Blumenherst was never obsessed with golf. She never even attended a golf academy and never practiced for long hours to the exclusion of everything else in her life. "My parents weren't trying to create a golfing phenom by having me on the range hitting balls every day," she said. She was dedicated, though; only once in her four years of high school did she miss a workout.

Neither is Blumenherst an erudite golf scholar. "I'm one of the most illiterate people when it comes to golf swings," she said. "I don't really know anything about golf swings. I just hit the ball."

Amanda Blumenherst keeps it simple.

Perhaps the simple life in America was doomed forever by the arrival of the programmable VCR, itself rendered defunct by more sophisticated technology. Since then, we've been on what seems to be an inevitably downward spiral into ever more complicated lives. Windshield wipers have multiple settings now, and washing machines have more options than cockpits do.

But we might do well in our own lives to mimic Amanda Blumenherst's simple approach to golf. That is, we should approach our lives with the keen awareness that success requires simplicity, a sticking to the basics: Revere God, love our families, honor our country, do our best.

Theologians may make what God did in Jesus as complicated as quantum mechanics and the infield fly rule, but God kept it simple for us: believe, trust, and obey. Believe in Jesus as the Son of God, trust that through him God makes possible our deliverance from our sins into Heaven, and obey God in the way he wants us to live. It's simple, but it's the true winning formula, the way to win for all eternity.

I think God made it simple. Just accept Him and believe.
— Bobby Bowden

Life continues to get ever more complicated,
but God made it simple for us
when he showed up as Jesus.

CHANGING TIMES

Read Hebrews 13:5-16.

"Jesus Christ is the same yesterday and today and forever" (v. 8).

The changing landscape of college basketball hit the Blue Devils especially hard after the 1999 season. So they simply went right on doing what they do best: winning.

Unlike many other schools, Duke had managed over the years to hang onto its superstars like Mike Gminski, Johnny Dawkins, Danny Ferry, Christian Laettner, Bobby Hurley, and Grant Hill for the full four years. After the 37-2 season of 1999, though, that all changed when sophomore center Elton Brand, the National Player of the Year, announced he was turning pro.

Brand left with Mike Krzyzewski's blessing, which softened the blow somewhat, but he was nevertheless the first Duke player to leave early. "I could understand Elton's situation," Coach K said. "He had missed a lot of time as a freshman with a broken foot, and the risk of something like that happening again was hanging over him."

What happened next was not with Coach K's blessing or his approval. Sophomore William Avery and freshman Corey Maggette surprised everyone by announcing they, too, were leaving Duke to turn pro. "It hurt my feelings a little bit," the coach said of the duo's departure. "There was no way I could have forecast that [Maggette and Avery] would leave."

BLUE DEVILS

But Krzyzewski understood that these were changing times for college basketball, and he and his coaches would just have to adjust. With the loss of so many players (another transferred), most pundits predicted a down year for Duke. Instead, they went 15-1 in the ACC and 29-5 overall and advanced to the Sweet 16.

Like everything else, college basketball has changed. Laptops and smart phones, high definition TVs, the Internet, and IMAX theaters — they and much that is in your life now may not have even been around when you were 16. Or even a decade ago. Consider how clothing styles, cars, communications, music, and tax laws constantly change.

Don't be too harsh on the world, though, because you' have changed also. You've aged, gained or lost weight, gotten married, changed jobs, or relocated.

Have you ever found yourself bewildered by the rapid pace of change, casting about for something to hold on to that will always be the same, that you can use as an anchor for your life? Is there anything like that?

Sadly, the answer's no. All the things of this world change.

On the other hand, there's Jesus, who is the same today, the same forever, always dependable, always loving you. No matter what happens in your life, Jesus is still the same.

Realistically, I'm not shocked by anything that happens in sport. It's a changing time and things like this will happen.
  — Mike Krzyzewski on three of his players turning pro

**In our ever-changing and bewildering world,
Jesus is the same forever;
his love for you will never change.**

DEAD WRONG

Read Matthew 26:14-16; 27:1-10.

"When Judas, who had betrayed him, saw that Jesus was condemned, he was seized with remorse" (v. 27:3).

Dick Groat was so good his senior season that some writers in the national media accused Duke of padding his statistics. They were wrong.

Groat came to Duke in 1948, one of the first four players ever to receive a basketball scholarship from the school. He started his junior season of 1950-51 by scoring 31 points, breaking the school record of 30 set by Duke's first two-time All-America, Ed Koffenberger. This was the first of an incredible nine times that season that the 6-foot guard broke the record. He averaged 25.2 points per game for that 20-13 team, almost doubling the school record for points in a season (831 to Koffenberer's 416) and leading the nation in scoring.

As a senior in 1951-52, Groat was even better. He averaged 26 points and 7.6 assists per game. Both numbers were second in the nation. For much of the season, Groat led the country in both categories, which led some writers to wonder how anybody could lead the country in these two seemingly mutually exclusive categories. Even the local papers were suspicious; *The Raleigh Times* asserted that the statistics at Duke were being padded.

As it turned out, both Groat and the school had a chance to demonstrate their integrity. The Blue Devils played back-to-back games at New York's Madison Square Garden and at the Palestra in Philadelphia, the most famous arenas in the country at the time. Duke beat NYU 74-72 and Temple 86-65. The official scorekeepers had Groat with ten and nine assists respectively, the latter a Palestra record. The Duke scorekeeper had Groat with one fewer assist in each game.

One sportswriter who had questioned Groat's ability wrote that he had been wrong, that Groat was indeed as remarkable a player as his statistics rightfully indicated.

There's wrong, there's dead wrong, and there's Judas wrong. We've all been wrong in our lives, but we can at least honestly ease our conscience by telling ourselves we'll never be as wrong as Judas was. A close examination of Judas' actions, however, reveals that we can indeed replicate in our own lives the mistake Judas made that drove him to suicidal despair.

Judas ultimately regretted his betrayal of our Lord, but his sorrow and remorse, however boundless, could not save him. His attempt to undo his initial wrong was futile because he tried to fix everything himself rather than turning to God in repentance and begging for mercy.

While we can't literally betray Jesus to his enemies as Judas did, we can match Judas' failure in our own lives by not turning to God in Jesus' name and asking for forgiveness for our sins. In that case, we ultimately will be as dead wrong as Judas was.

We made too many wrong mistakes.

— *Yogi Berra*

A sin is the first wrong; failing to ask God
for forgiveness of it is the second.

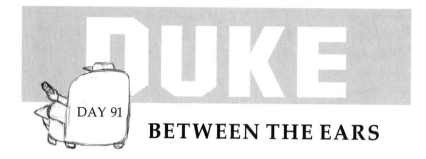

BETWEEN THE EARS

Read Philippians 4:4-9.

"Do not be anxious about anything, . . . And the God of peace will be with you" (vv. 6a, 9b).

The difference that led to one of the biggest wins in the David Cutcliffe era didn't lie in the physical punishment Duke handed out. Rather, the winning edge came because the Blue Devils were mentally tough.

Oct. 26, 2013, saw what has become a typical game for Duke against Virginia Tech in Blacksburg. The Blue Devils had never won there. Moreover, the Hokies were ranked 16th in the nation, and Duke had not beaten a ranked team on the road since 1971.

And what transpired was pretty ugly. Anthony Boone was only 7-for-25 passing for 107 yards, no touchdowns, and four interceptions. Duke didn't complete a pass in the second half. The offense went 0-for-11 on third downs and was outgained 387 yards to 198. Tech had the ball for more than 39 minutes.

This night, though, that could have seen another devastating defeat instead saw a "historic upset" that was deemed "pivotal" to the program. This night was different; Duke won 13-10.

How in the world? The Blue Devils played the way their head coach said they had to to win: mentally tough. Not just for sixty minutes, he said, but "in between plays, at halftime, it all counts."

Boone ran for a touchdown and knew exactly where the down marker was late in the game, battling his way to a first down that

BLUE DEVILS

let the offense run out the clock. The defense picked off four passes and didn't break down the stretch after holding Tech scoreless in the first half. Ross Martin became the first major-college kicker of the season to boot two 50+-yard field goals in the same game.

The Blue Devils were tough enough all right, but not just physically. They also had the toughness right between their ears.

Away from the sports arena, persevering in American society today generally necessitates mental strength, which, as the Blue Devils illustrated in their win over Virginia Tech, is even harder to attain than physical prowess.

Your job, your family, your finances, just getting everything done every day — they all demand mental toughness from you by placing stress upon you to perform. Stress is a fact of life, though it isn't all bad as you are often led to believe. Stress can lead you to function at your best. Rather than buckling under it, you stand up, make constant decisions, and keep going.

So it is with your faith life. "Too blessed to be stressed" sounds nice, but followers of Jesus Christ know all about stress. Society screams compromise; your children whine about being cool; your company ignores ethics. But you don't fold beneath the stress; you keep your mind on Christ and the way he said to live because you are tough mentally, strengthened by your faith.

After all, you have God's word and God's grace for relief and support.

You're going to have to be mentally tough the entire time.
— *David Cutcliffe to his team before the Va. Tech game*

**Toughened mentally by your faith in Christ,
you live out what you believe, and you persevere.**

DUKE

A Note or Two from the Author to the Fans of the Blue Devils

My passion is for the college games, a situation that -- alas -- each winter throws me into the depths of despair and depression. I am a Georgia Bulldog, and over the decades UGA's basketball program has -- with a consistency they couldn't achieve if they tried -- been miserable, ranking right up there (or right down there) with such epic failures as the Titanic, George Armstrong Custer, and the Edsel.

Thus, once the last touchdown is scored in the January bowl games, I have virtually nothing to cheer for until the first pitches of the collegiate baseball/softball seasons. I do manage to watch a little of the NCAA Tournament, but only half-heartedly, since Georgia rarely qualifies.

Thus, I confess to you, oh fans of the mighty Blue Devils, each winter I succumb to one of the Seven Deadly Sins: I envy you your basketball success.

It's a good thing my identity and my sense of well-being do not lie in being a college basketball fan -- or a Georgia Bulldog. I am first and foremost a Christian. My true identity lies in Jesus Christ, my Lord and Savior. Through him, I am a child of God and an heir to a kingdom.

Many of the identities we don during our lives are temporary; they change with our circumstances over the years. Once we accept Jesus, though, we are children of God. He has promised, and one thing the Bible teaches us is that God doesn't renege on his promises.

BLUE DEVILS

All my adult life, the only goal I sought was to write a book and have it published and sell a few copies. Several years ago, I surrendered that goal at the same time that I surrendered my life to God, telling him to do what he would. To my stupefaction, he called me into the ministry.

Thereupon I set out upon the most glorious time of my life. Every day was a miracle as I continually left my proverbial comfort zone far behind and discovered that which makes a life truly worth living: serving God. As it turned out, only when I set my personal goal aside and instead devoted my life to God's purposes for me did he hand me everything of which I had dreamed. And so we have this book and more than thirty others.

I suggest you try it, this difficult surrendering stuff. Each one of us has a ministry God has placed upon us. It may not be full-time ministry, especially pulpit ministry. Only you can know the way in which God is speaking to your heart. I can only give you my example to help you decide. From my whole heart, I tell you to go for it.

If you're reading this page, then you've read the book. My fondest prayer for these devotions is that they offer you some enjoyment, recall a few precious memories for you, draw a smile or two, and provide a little insight into and depth for your faith.

Have fun! Have faith! Go Blue Devils! Go God!

Ed McMinn

NOTES
(by Devotion Day Number)

1 Football, track and field, . . . them all to Trinity University.: Bill Brill, *Duke Basketball: One Hundred Seasons* (Champaign, IL: Sports Publishing L.L.C., 2004), p. 29.

1 Card arrived at Trinity . . . Card simply organized one.: Brill, p. 29.

1 "unlike baseball, the game is played most often at night.": Brill, p. 30.

1 "one of the most fascinating . . . indoor sports known today.": Brill, p. 29.

1 Iron guards were fastened . . . constructed and attached.: Brill, p. 30.

1 none of whom had ever . . . practiced three weeks: Brill, p. 31.

1 Only about one-third . . . from one end to the other.: Brill, p. 30.

1 It is well-nigh a certainty . . . The game is basketball.: Brill, p. 29.

2 Duke Athletic Director Bill Butters asked . . . the head coach at West Point: Mike Krzyzewski.: Brill, p. 81.

2 Reluctant to commit to . . . wasn't of ACC caliber,: Dick Weiss, *True Blue* (Champaign, IL: Sports Publishing L.L.C., 2005), p. 4.

2 Shortly after the coach . . . "You'll be fair.": Weiss, p. 5.

2 when the man who would be . . . We didn't discuss it.": Brill, p. 82.

3 he would lose five to ten pounds per practice.: A.J. Carr, "Twice the Work, Twice the Payoff," *The News & Observer*, Aug. 21, 2007.

3 "The football team plus academics brought me here.": "Patrick Bailey '08," *Office of News & Communications: Duke University*, Nov. 27, 2006, http://www.dukenews.duke.edu/2006/11/bailey.html, July 6, 2010.

3 "Shoot," he said, letting . . . a big part of my life.": "Patrick Bailey '08."

3 I wanted to get that shot . . . the best of what chance I have.: "Duke Rush End Patrick Bailey Has Signed a Free Agent Contract with the NFL's Pittsburgh Steelers," *The Devil's Den*, April 29, 2008, http://duke.scout.com/2/751036.html, July 6, 2010.

4 In a survey on Match.com . . . would kill the deal.: Robbi Pickeral, "Duke Plays Familiar Role Again: the Villain," *The News & Observer*, April 3, 2010.

4 The week of the game . . . might influence games.": Pickeral, "Duke Plays."

4 If we're going to . . . That's your problem.: Pickeral, "Duke Plays."

5 Duke-Kentucky was the greatest college game of them all.": Bob

Ryan as quoted in Brill, p. 127.

5 "We're going to win . . . Hill fired a strike.: Brill, p. 126.

5 Laettner had time to . . . shot in collegiate history.": Brill, pp. 126-27.

5 No other college game . . . and this much drama.: Brill, p. 127.

6 It spoke to her . . . Maybe I can do it.": Edward G. Robinson III, "Harding Returns to Duke to Have Jersey Retired," *The News & Observer*, Jan. 20, 2008.

6 "had the best senior season . . . history of women's basketball.: Robinson, "Harding Returns."

6 It's overwhelming. . . . to be there forever.: Robinson, "Harding Returns."

7 UNC comptroller Billy Carmichael . . . lens that never moved.: Art Chansky, *Blue Blood* (New York City: Thomas Dunne Books, 2006), p. 53.

7 Duke rallied from an eight-point . . . to tie the game at 73.: Chansky, p. 53.

7 After his last basket, . . . the score was tied.: Chansky, pp. 53-54.

7 UNC didn't beat us. Their scorekeeper did.: Chansky, p. 54.

8 "brought a warrior mentality to the court." "Nate James Bio," *GoDuke.com*, May 6, 2008, http://www.goduke.com/View Article.dbml?DB_OEM_ID=4200&ATCLID=1458688, July 19, 2010.

8 the "leatherneck attitude" . . . like [physically] at a different level.": A.J. Carr, "Mr. Tough Guy," *The News & Observer*, Jan. 29, 2000, p. 1C.

8 Late in James' senior year, . . . find a kid like that?": Grant Wahl, "The Duke Way," *Sports Illustrated*, Nov. 21, 2005, http://sportsillustrated.cnn.com/vault/article/magazine/MAG1113830/index.htm, July 19, 2010.

8 One of the attributes . . . was his toughness.: "Nate James Bio."

8 Ask him to run through a wall and he would do it.: Carr, "Mr. Tough Guy."

9 he became the first active . . . cover of *Sports Illustrated*.: Alwyn Featherston, *Game of My Life: Duke* (Champaign, IL: Sports Publishing L.L.C., 2007), p. 63.

9 Banks prayed, "God, give . . . with a good memory.": Featherston, p. 66.

9 Banks had often thrown roses to the crowd in high school,: Featherston, p. 66.

9 he took a rose to . . . already sky-high crowd.: Jim Sumner, *Tales from the Duke Blue Devils Hardwood*

(Champaign, IL: Sports Publishing, L.L.C., 2005), p. 112.

9 "That's when it kicked in . . . would lose this game.": Featherston, p. 67.

9 the frenzied students carried . . . ever been to heaven,": Sumner, *Tales from the Duke Blue Devils Hardwood*, p. 113.

10 Duke coach Bill Murray kept telling . . . would come their way.: Jim Sumner, "1954 [*sic*] Orange Bowl: Duke 34, Nebraska 7," *GoDuke.com*, Oct. 2, 2004, http://www.goduke.com/ViewArticle. dbml?&DB_OEM_ID=4200, July 14, 2010.

10 "My friends said I should have . . . knew I had been hit.": Sumner, "1954 [*sic*] Orange Bowl."

11 when Duke hosted Wake . . . confined to quarters.": Brill, p. 39.

11 Wartime gas rationing also limited the turnout.: Brill, p. 40.

11 He also worked as . . . resort in the summer.: Brill, p. 38.

11 Gerard missed the game . . . no problem with it either.: Brill, p. 39.

12 Point guard Bobby Hurley was . . . being chased by sharks.: Jim Sumner, *Tales from the Duke Blue Devils Hardwood*, p. 140.

12 Emily Krzyzewski sought to . . . played for the national championship.": Bill Brill and Mike Krzyzewski, *A Season Is a Lifetime* (New York City: Simon & Schuster, 1993), p. 65.

12 "widely hailed as the best . . . afraid of anything or anybody.": Jim Sumner, *Tales from the Duke Blue Devils Hardwood*, p. 145.

12 "See, Mike, I told you that you'd do better this time.": Brill and Krzyzewski, p. 65.

13 When the team boarded the bus . . . when we win the national championship.": Mike Krzyzewski, with Donald T. Phillips, *Five-Point Play* (New York City: Warner Books, Inc., 2001), p. 185.

13 After the post-game interviews . . . strut down the aisle.": Krzyzewski with Phillips, p. 226.

14 "As a competitor," . . . you're up to the task.": Laura Keeley, "Duke Ready for 'Greatest Challenge,'" *The News & Observer*, Nov. 25, 2013, http://nl.newsbank.com/nl-search/we/Archives?p_ action=doc&p_docid=14A55A7636A4B948.

14 defensive linemen Sydney . . . what we've just done.": "No. 24 Duke Beats North Carolina," *Sports Illustrated*, Nov. 30, 2013, http:// sportsillustrated.cnn.com/football/ncaa/gameflash/2013/11/30/ 53985/index.html.

14 No question, this is our greatest challenge.: Keeley, "Duke Ready for 'Greatest Challenge.'"

15 Both Wake Forest and . . . frozen the ball against Duke.: Brill, p. 57.

15   "Compared with what was to . . . was a shootout.": Brill, p. 57.

15   As the last half proceeded . . . It's always pennies, never quarters,":
     Brill, p. 57.

16   The play called for Collins . . . which "bounced around and
     bounced off.": Sumner, *Tales from the Duke Blue Devils Hard-
     wood*, p. 159.

16   Wojciechowski had a great view . . . sure that Marshall's shot was
     in.": Sumner, *Tales from the Duke Blue Devils Hardwood*, p. 159.

17   I don't remember getting tired. I never thought about it.": Jim Sum-
     ner, "Sixty-Minute Man," *GoDuke.com*, July 26, 2004, http://
     www.goduke.com/ViewArticle.dbml?&DB_OEM_ID=4200,
     July 14, 2010.

17   Clark arrived in Durham . . . crediting a block from Tom Davis.:
     Sumner, "Sixty-Minute Man."

17   You were just prepared . . . the coaches asked you to.: Sumner,
     "Sixty-Minute Man."

18   Williams struggled to adjust . . . like that in basketball.": Feather-
     ston, p. 186.

18   "It was, in fact, too much . . . to that atmosphere.": Featherston,
     p. 186.

19   Nobody foresaw Edwards' explosive performance against N.C.
     State.: Danielle Lazarus, "DeVon Edwards Plays Unlikely Hero
     for Duke Football," *The Chronicle*, Nov. 11, 2013, http://www.
     dukechronicle.com/articles/2013/11/11/devon-edwards-plays-
     lunkely-hero-duke-football.

20   Duke had a lapse of . . . knew what was coming.: Chansky, p. 131.

21   When Jane Preyer became head . . . she secured the O'Reily trip-
     lets: Jim Sumner, "Looking Back: Duke's 13-Year Run in
     Women's Tennis, *TheACC.com*, May 5, 2009, http://www.theacc.
     com/sports/w-tennis/spec-rel/050509aaa.html, July 14, 2010.

21   "put Duke on the map. . . . the program around them.: Sumner,
     "Looking Back: Duke's 13-Year Run."

21   The goal of other ACC . . . competition is just too tough.: Sumner,
     "Looking Back: Duke's 13-Year Run."

21   Duke's 13-year dynasty was bigger . . . and it just fed off itself.:
     Sumner, "Looking Back: Duke's 13-Year Run."

22   Miles Plumlee couldn't get . . . high school in Indiana.: Ken Tysiac,
     "Devils Draw Inspiration," *The News & Observer*, April 5, 2010,
     p. 1C, http://nl.newsbank.com/nl-search/we/Archives?p_
     action=doc&p_docid=12F0E9005BE5A, July 22, 2010.

22   where the coach . . . to prove himself.: Tysiac, "Devils

Draw Inspiration."
22 "skilled at creating offense . . . father used to tell him.: Tysiac, "Devils Draw Inspiration."
22 turned to his mother . . . backbone through everything.": Tysiac, "Devils Draw Inspiration."
22 He credited his . . . there for support,": Tysiac, "Devils Draw Inspiration."
23 The Devils didn't have enough . . . look particularly physical.: Brill, p. 89.
23 "This team is out to prove . . . I think they can do it.": Brill, p. 89.
23 Duke was the most experienced team in the country,: Brill, p. 88.
23 They will go down as the greatest not-great team ever.: Brill, p. 89.
24 "The wisest and most . . . to solve Duke's performance.": Sumner, *Tales from the Duke Blue Devils Hardwood*, p. 9.
24 "Duke was a football . . . give basketball some recognition.": Sumner, *Tales from the Duke Blue Devils Hardwood*, p. 10.
24 Bill Werber and Harry . . . passive the rest of [the] game.": Sumner, *Tales from the Duke Blue Devils Hardwood*, p. 7.
25 It's been tough times for us,": Tom Harris, "Blue Devils Come Alive in Death Valley," *The News & Observer*, Oct. 19, 1980, p. 1-II.
25 It is a great, great victory for us.: Harris.
26 It was a discouraged bunch . . . at the Charlotte Coliseum.: Brill and Krzyzewski, p. 17.
26 he walked to the back . . . set the tone for everyone.: Brill and Krzyzewski, p. 20.
26 "We're going to win . . . was now NCAA time.: Brill and Krzyzewski, p. 20.
26 when they had hoped for . . . had been dispelled.": Brill and Krzyzewski, pp. 20-21.
27 Bubas spent hours watching . . . learned from all that study.: Frank Deford "A Lost Weekend in Carolina," *Sports Illustrated*, Dec. 20, 1965, http://sportsillustrated.cnn.com/vault/article/magazine/MAG1078028/index.htm, July 3, 2010.
27 The coach saw that the . . . six-man scrub team.: Deford.
27 Only six times in 75 . . . before Duke cleared midcourt.: Deford.
28 "We've been waiting . . . all came together today.": Joe Tiede, "Emotions and Points Flow as Duke Completes Mission," *The News & Observer*, Nov. 19, 1989, p. 8B.
28 "ever been on or coached, . . . every one of them.": Tiede, "Emotions and Points Flow."
29 "could have swallowed kryptonite.": Sumner, *Tales from the Duke*

Blue Devils Hardwood, p. 135.

29 He then seriously considered . . . so I decided to stay.": Featherston, p. 97.

29 Ferry saw little need . . . gave in and served pancakes.: Featherston, p. 98.

29 "It was totally in a zone," . . . See ball, catch ball, shoot ball.": Sumner, *Tales from the Duke Blue Devils Hardwood*, p. 134.

29 Something divine was . . . could have swallowed kryptonite tonight.": Sumner, *Tales from the Duke Blue Devils Hardwood*, p. 135.

29 I guess we'll have pancakes more often.: Featherston, p. 99.

30 by November he was too . . . the little-known coach: Brill, p. 42.

30 "We never gave that . . . well in the Dixie Classic.": Brill, p. 41.

30 At one point he scored . . . Dayton Allen hit a layup: Brill, p. 41.

30 Make it a little respectable.: Brill, p. 41.

31 How the name arose is lost to history,: Brill, p. 102.

31 in the 1970s Maryland . . . Terps were shooting layups.: Brill, p. 102.

31 the attention paid to them by the everlastingly exuberant Dick Vitale,: Brill, p. 102.

31 In 1986, announcer and . . . peanuts to the crowd.: Brill, p. 103.

31 Coach Mike Krzyzewski has . . . than abuse an opponent.: Brill, p. 103.

31 one Crazy stood as . . . of Speedo Guy was born.: Brill, pp. 103-04.

32 From Alsace, France, Vernerey played . . . and holiday family time.: Edward G. Robinson III, "Duke Women's Import Has Polish," *The News & Observer*, Dec. 24, 2009.

33 Brand "was an immediate force": Weiss, p. 195.

33 "was the dominant force . . . was Coach K's practices.": Weiss, p. 196.

33 His mom kept him off . . . picked up on his own.: Weiss, p. 194.

33 His natural inclination was . . . you're going to play.": Weiss, p. 194.

34 As the run rose over . . . at least for 12 months.": Eric Ferreri, "Life Is Sweeter at the Top for Duke Blue Devils," *The News & Observer*, April 7, 2010.

34 "to an inglorious second- . . . the 15-501 seesaw was intoxicating.: Ferreri.

34 "It's definitely a little . . . was the runner-up in the NIT,": Ferreri.

34 Hoarse from his weekend . . . we won together this year.": Ferreri.

35 I couldn't believe it, touchdown after touchdown.: A.J. Carr, "Duke Erupts for 34 First-Quarter Points," *The News & Observer*, Nov. 14, 1999, p. 1CC.

36   "stunned the basketball world": Sumner, *Tales from the Duke Blue Devils Hardwood*, p. 79.

36   Duke athletic director Eddie . . . ten finalists for the job.: Sumner, *Tales from the Duke Blue Devils Hardwood*, p. 39.

36   "Duke has secured an . . . to direct its program.": Sumner, *Tales from the Duke Blue Devils Hardwood*, p. 41.

36   Gentlemen, this is Vic Bubas, . . . is our coach forever.: Sumner, *Tales from the Duke Blue Devils Hardwood*, p. 40.

36   He called each of his . . . time to do something else.": Sumner, *Tales from the Duke Blue Devils Hardwood*, p. 79.

36   [Coach Bubas] told us that . . . to continue like that.: Sumner, *Tales from the Duke Blue Devils Hardwood*, p. 79.

37   After an incident at Cameron . . . the "Uncle Terry letter.": Sumner, *Tales from the Duke Blue Devils Hardwood*, p. 120.

37   He called on the Cameron Crazies . . . in this league, all right?": Sumner, *Tales from the Duke Blue Devils Hardwood*, p. 121.

37   "had publicly put a dunce cap on Dean Smith's head": Gregg Doyel, *Coach K* (Lenexa, KS: Addax Publishing Group, Inc., 1999), p. 81.

38   "That made me think . . . a lot more attractive.": Jim Sumner, "Looking Back: Patience Paid Off for Duke's Anthony Dilweg," *TheACC.com*, Sept. 17, 2008, http://www.theacc.com/sports/m-footbl/spec-rel/091708aad.html, July 14, 2010.

38   Dilweg saw the combination . . . I like that,": Sumner, "Looking Back: Patience Paid Off."

38   Now I've done it. How do I get out of this mess?: Sumner, "Looking Back: Patience Paid Off."

39   the team returned to their . . . adult cry before: Brill and Krzyzewski, p. 15.

39   his mother, who cried when he chose Duke over UNC: Jeff Eisenberg, "Christian Laettner's Mom Cried When He Chose Duke over UNC," *rivals.com*, June 30, 2008, http://rivals.yahoo.com/ncaa/basketball/blog/the_dagger/post/Christian-Laettner-s-mom, July 21, 2010.

39   It was difficult for me . . . did Laettner leave the room.: Brill and Kryyzewski, p. 15.

39   I will always remember . . . better than any victory.: Brill and Krzyzewski, p. 15.

40   "The Devils obviously looked like anything but champions.": Brill, p. 50.

40   "We have been manhandled . . . out there and play basketball.":

Brill, p. 50.

40   When you get down to realism, . . . had gone to San Francisco.:
     Brill, p. 51.

40   "despicable, vile, unprincipled scoundrels.": John MacArthur,
     Twelve Ordinary Men (Nashville: W Publishing Group, 2002),
     p. 152.

41   "My knees were shaking before the game,": Joe Tiede, "TD Pass on
     First Play Calmed Brown's Nerves," *The News & Observer*, Nov.
     5, 1989, p. 14B.

41   since the Virginia game . . . What if it's intercepted?": Tiede, "TD
     Pass on First Play."

41   Spurrier helped his rookie . . . faked to tailback Randy Cuthbert:
     Tiede, "TD Pass on First Play."

42   playing basketball on a dirt court with her parents and older sib-
     lings.: Kelli Anderson, "Devil's Due," *Sports Illustrated*, Nov. 25,
     2002, http://sportsillustrated.cnn.com/vault/article/magazine/
     MAG1027611/index.htm, July 19, 2010.

42   Tennessee and Connecticut were . . . doomed UT's chances.:
     Anderson.

42   An associate coach mistakenly . . . Huskies never even called.:
     Anderson.

42   Head coach Gail Goestenkors . . . player I've ever seen.": Anderson.

42   Coach Pat Summitt glares . . . name comes up.: Anderson.

43   Duke Stadium was the first facility . . . after a 24-year ban.: "Wal-
     lace Wade Stadium," *Duke University Libraries: University
     Archives*, http://library.duke.edu/uarchives/history/histnotes/
     wade_stadium.html, July 27, 2010.

43   In the wake of the bombing . . .not been played in Pasadena.:
     "Duke Football Timeline: 1942 Rose Bowl Game," *Pursuit of
     Excellence: 2009 Duke Football*, p. 171, http://www.goduke.com/
     ViewArticle.dbml.

43   In honor of the displaced . . . at the stadium entrance.: "Wallace
     Wade Stadium," *Pursuit of Excellence: 2009 Duke Football*, p. 42.
     http://www.goduke.com/ViewArticle.dbml.

44   Krzyzewski always identified at least . . . performance and
     achievement.": Krzyzewski with Phillips, p. 5.

44   Krzyzewski and his wife, . . . in Hawaii prior to the season.:
     Krzyzewski with Phillips, p. 6.

44   When Williams stepped away . . . for attention this year?"
     Krzyzewski with Phillips, p. 7.

44   Battier could have been . . . the conversation to himself:

Krzyzewski with Phillips, pp. 7-8.

44 "That's our senior leader. Honest. No jealousy. Rock solid.":
Krzyzewski with Phillips, p. 8.

44 "ambivalent, vacillating, impulsive, unsubmissive." MacArthur,
p. 39.

44 "the greatest preacher . . . the "dominant figure": MacArthur, p. 39.

45 "We'll be experimenting . . . is done by committee,": Brill, p. 132.

45 only seven players saw much action.: Brill, p. 135.

45 "I'm still working on the . . . pass the ball to himself,": Brill, p. 133.

45 "We went absolutely as far as we could,": Brill, p. 135.

45 I thought we did a lot . . . forward or much depth.: Brill, p. 135.

46 When head coach David Cutcliffe . . . that he was still here.":
Edward G. Robinson III, "Duke's Lewis Leaves His Mark,"
The News & Observer, Nov. 27, 2009.

46 "The easy way out . . . seriously thought about leaving;: Robinson,
"Duke's Lewis Leaves His Mark."

46 actually started out as . . . words often turned to fisticuffs.": Robinson, "Duke's Lewis Leaves His Mark."

46 Where [Thaddeus Lewis] is from, . . . fight out of a losing tradition.:
Robinson, "Duke's Lewis Leaves His Mark."

47 They saw something no one . . . overseas trips could be made.:
Brill, p. 171.

48 Armstrong spent most of his . . . had a player work harder.": Sumner, *Tales from the Duke Blue Devils Hardwood*, p. 91.

48 though many of his shots . . . getting him a new arm,": Sumner,
Tales from the Duke Blue Devils Hardwood, p. 92.

48 receiving votes for the top 20 . . . fell hard on his right wrist.: Sumner, *Tales from the Duke Blue Devils Hardwood*, p. 95.

48 When trainer Max Crowder . . . to get me off the court.": Sumner,
Tales from the Duke Blue Devils Hardwood, p. 95.

48 I knew right away I had broken it. The pain was intense.: Sumner,
Tales from the Duke Blue Devils Hardwood, p. 95.

49 "The coaching change that would . . . that it remains today": Brill,
33.

49 the university's vice-president . . . academy in West Virginia: Brill,
p. 33.

50 Sime came to Durham in 1954 . . . he gave up athletics.: Jim Sumner, "Looking Back: Duke Track & Field Sensation Dave Sime,"
TheACC.com, April 16, 2008, http://www.theacc.com/sports/c-
track/spec-rel/041608aaa.html, July 14, 2010.

51 On May 6, the day . . . from North Carolina to Duke.: Brill, p. 48.

51   Brown took offense at . . . in a couple of minutes,: Brill, p. 52.

51   "Duke was never the same after that.": Brill, p. 51.

52   "one of the most solid and respected programs in the country."
     Featherston, p. 2.

52   "This guy was always . . . sudden, he's breaking down.": Featherston, p. 4.

52   to disappearing at the end of the bench.: Featherston, p. 4.

52   I felt hurt because . . . a team losing that many games.: Featherston,
     p. 4.

53   "first foray on the recruiting . . . less than a disaster.": Featherston,
     p. 71.

53   most of the success . . . world of big-time recruiting.": Featherston,
     p. 71.

53   "the inexperienced Duke coach couldn't close the deal.": Featherston, p. 71.

53   He would fly across . . . Nobody knew who he was.": Weiss, p. 28.

53   "the recruit who would make his program.": Featherston, p. 74.

54   Jean Berry and Art Gregory, . . . We just knew,": Jim Sumner,
     "Looking Back: A Look Inside Duke's Gridiron Success in the
     Early 1960's," *TheACC.com*, Sept. 26, 2006, http://www.theacc.
     com/genrel/092606aaf.html, July 14, 2010.

54   bowl officials dawdled for a week,: Sumner, "Looking Back: A
     Look Inside."

54   some of the players didn't want . . . But he didn't.": Sumner, "Look-
     ing Back: A Look Inside."

54   It was the right decision. . . . It just wasn't right.: Sumner, "Looking
     Back: A Look Inside."

55   "I heard something pop,": Brill and Krzyzewski, p. 171.

55   the crowd "went bonkers" . . . went into the game.: Brill and
     Krzyzewski, p. 198.

55   With seconds left in . . . with a severe cramp.: Brill and Krzyzew-
     ski, p. 198.

55   after the game ended, . . . with the game ball: Brill and Krzyzew-
     ski, p. 199.

56   the game was tied at 30 with under eight minutes to go in the
     half.: Sumner, *Tales from the Duke Blue Devils Hardwood*, p. 168.

56   flattened with a forearm blow . . . It was show no mercy.": Sumner,
     Tales from the Duke Blue Devils Hardwood, p. 168.

56   Langdon received some stitches,: Sumner, *Tales from the Duke
     Blue Devils Hardwood*, p. 168.

56   "a purely selfish matter . . . unwelcome misfortune or

frustration": Bruce T. Dahlberg, "Anger," *The Interpreter's Dictionary of the Bible* (Nashville: Abingdon Press, 1962), Vol. 1, p. 136.

56   My captain was lying . . . needs to sit in the chair.: Sumner, *Tales from the Duke Blue Devils Hardwood*, p. 168.

57   "They played us well.": Featherston, p. 78.

57   As a largely passive Greensboro crowd: Featherston, p. 78.

57   State led 44-37 with 12 minutes left to play.: Featherston, p. 79.

57   "I can remember thinking . . . we were losing to this team,": Featherston, p. 78.

57   "I still believe that this day,": p. 79.

57   That game was a . . . was its own entity.": Featherston, p. 80.

58   When Pierce was a freshman in . . . was the petition's instigator.: Michelle Gardner, "No Mama's Boy," *South Florida Sun Sentinel*, Oct. 23, 1996, http://article.sun-sentinel.com/1996-10-23/news/9610220681_1, July 13, 2010.

58   Pierce's football success led him . . . from Coach Fred Goldsmith.: A.J. Carr, "Pierce Overcomes Family Tragedy," *The News & Observer*, Sept. 2, 1999, p. 6C.

58   He was everything I want to be.: Carr, "Pierce Overcomes Family Tragedy."

59   Duke head coach Vic . . . all-around player of his era.: Featherston, p. 14.

59   Marin was a nationally . . . of a commitment.: Featherston, p. 14.

59   when the Pitt coach failed . . . cold and foggy and drizzling.": Featherston, p. 16.

59   A significant part of my decision had to do with weather.: Featherston, p. 16.

60   "In the past, I've just . . . and so did the team.": Brill, p. 74.

60   by switching to a spread offense . . . an 18-2 run over seven minutes: Brill, p. 75.

60   The Penn coach said . . . hurt them against Villanova.": Brill, p. 75.

60   Our guys were really . . . about all that stuff that's been written.: Brill, p. 75.

61   It will forever be known as the 'Miracle Minute.'": Brill, p. 160.

61   ESPN conceded a Maryland . . . Player of the Game.: Krzyzewski with Phillips, p. 85.

61   With 61 seconds left, . . . second-ranked Blue Devils.: Brill, p. 160.

61   "They had done an extraordinary thing,": Krzyzewski, with Phillips, p. 88.

61   We're going to come back . . . about his game forever.: Krzyzewski

with Phillips, p. 85.

62   "were trapped in a . . . sport to be dropped.: Caulton Tudor, "Blue
      Devils Make Statement," *The News & Observer,* June 1, 2010.

62   "The scars on the program . . . competition could be restored.":
      Tudor, "Blue Devils Make Statement."

62   "Duke's bid for the ultimate . . . the spirit of [the] program.": Tudor,
      "Blue Devils Make Statement."

62   It's definitely relief. It's like an epiphany.: Patrick Stevens, "Costa-
      bile Supplies Clincher for Devils," *The News & Observer,* June 1,
      2010.

63   "mild-mannered 'gentleman coach,'": Brill, p. 43.

63   His first practice didn't . . . didn't know what to think.: Brill, p. 43.

63   "We had never heard of him," . . . no idea who he was.: Sumner,
      Tales from the Duke Blue Devils Hardwood, p. 20.

63   "He told us he wanted . . . at him like he was crazy.": Sumner, *Tales
      from the Duke Blue Devils Hardwood,* p. 20.

63   He pointed out to his players . . . 85.2 points per game: Sumner,
      Tales from the Duke Blue Devils Hardwood, p. 20.

63   We just ran and ran. . . . other team with their pants down.: Sum-
      ner, *Tales from the Duke Blue Devils Hardwood,* p. 20.

64   the pundits said Duke was . . . which clanged out.: Robbi Pickeral,
      "Devils Drive Away Doubters," *The News & Observer,* April 6,
      2010, p. 5C, http://nl.newsbank.com.nl-search/we/Archives?p_
      action=doc&p_docid=12F0E902D097A, July 22, 2010.

65   "It's unbelievable." "It hasn't sunk in yet, but it's unbelievable.":
      "National Champions!" *GoDuke.com,* May 20, 2009, http://
      www.goduke.com/ViewArticle.dbml?DB_OEM_ID=4200&
      ATCLID=3740746, July 26, 2010.

65   "unbelievably resilient.": "National Champions!"

65   the player who clinched . . . up to me.": "National Champions!"

65   It's unbelievable. I . . . describe the feeling.: "National Champions!"

66   Eddie Cameron always insisted . . . a shot off in the air.": Brill, p. 36.

66   Werber arrived at Duke . . . trees and ivy walls." Brill, p. 36.

66   A railroad track ran . . . to pack up and go home.": Brill, p. 36.

66   Duke in September, 1926, was a sorry-looking place.: Brill, p. 36.

67   It went just like we planned.": Brill, p. 113.

67   "he never regained the . . . before getting hurt.": Brill, p. 111.

67   Maryland got the ball . . . "There is no explanation,": Brill, p. 112.

67   prompting a locker-room . . . and "too many quitters.": Brill,
      p. 112.

67   UCLA wiped out a . . . pray Phil would save us.": Brill,

p. 113.

68 In the spring of 1999, . . . Atlanta Church of Christ.: A.J. Carr, "Duke QB Ready for Long-Awaited Start," *The News & Observer*, Sept. 24, 1999, p. 6C.

68 He asked Thompson to consider . . . immersed himself in football.": Carr, "Duke QB Ready."

68 I was through with football.: Carr, "Duke QB Ready."

69 After changing planes several . . . "You better be good.": Sumner, *Tales from the Duke Blue Devils Hardwood*, p. 74.

69 "It was agonizing, watching . . . letting my team down.": Sumner, *Tales from the Duke Blue Devils Hardwood*, p. 76.

69 He made two free throws . . . into a second overtime.: Sumner, *Tales from the Duke Blue Devils Hardwood*, p. 76.

69 "It occurred to me that . . . tried to enjoy it.": Sumner, *Tales from the Duke Blue Devils Hardwood*, p. 76.

69 "It was almost surreal,": Jim Sumner, "Looking Back: A Triple Overtime Classic in the Duke-Carolina Rivalry," *TheACC.com*, Feb. 21, 2008, http://www.theacc.com/sports/m-baskbl/specrel/022108aac.html, July 20, 2010.

69 Like all reserves, . . . if I just had the chance.: Sumner, *Tales from the Duke Blue Devils Hardwood*, p. 76.

70 At Cole Field House, the teams . . . were the dejected Maryland players.: Brill and Krzyzewski, p. 144.

70 No wonder they hate us.: Brill and Krzyzewski, p. 145.

71 he told his team that had only one chance in a million: Caulton Tudor, "Stunned Tigers Say Blue Devils Simply Played 'a Lot Tougher,'" *The News & Observer*, Oct. 1, 1989, p. 9B.

71 Spurrier instructed his team . . . off the improbable upset.: Tudor, "Stunned Tigers,"

71 "Hardly anyone gave us . . . the rest of our lives.": Joe Tiede, "One in a Million -- 21-7," *The News & Observer*, Oct. 1, 1989, p. 1B.

71 It's amazing. Some of . . . of being a Christian man.: Bettinger, Jim & Julie S, *The Book of Bowden* (Nashville, TN: TowleHouse Publishing, 2001), p. 121.

72 Coach Bill Murray decided his . . . so they could practice.: Joe Tiede, "Duke's Road to 1961 Bowl Was a Cotton-Picking Grind," *The News & Observer*, Dec. 6, 1989, p. 1C.

73 "We stand alone,": A.J. Carr, "Duke Savors 28 Straight," *The News & Observer*, Jan. 23, 2000, p. 1C.

73 Carrawell said he couldn't . . . a conference game during the regular season.: Carr, "Duke Savors 28."

73 a small contingent of . . . as the clock wound down.: Carr, "Duke Savors 28."

73 a "terrific thing," but . . . it [is] truly remarkable.": Carr, "Duke Savors 28."

73 We want to keep it going.: Carr, "Duke Savors 28."

74 his defensive talents that . . . defense was ball pressure,": Featherston, p. 176.

74 "I was like the middle . . . n the right position.": Featherston, p. 177.

74 Temple Owls had only one scary offensive weapon:: Featherston, p. 178.

74 "Okay, Billy, you've . . . could shut him down.: Featherston, p. 178.

74 he broke down and cried.: Featherston, p. 179.

74   I never thought that . . . be a defensive guy.: Featherston, p. 176.

75 "we would have one . . . what I thought it would be.": Brill, p. 82.

75 People started howling again.: Weiss, p. 7.

75 "We've got a public who . . . I need to do it right now.": Weiss, p. 7.

75 You tell [everyone] you've . . . let's let the people know.: Weiss, p. 7.

76 "revolutionized the ACC at quarterback": Jim Sumner, "Looking Back: Duke's Leo Hart Revolutionized the ACC at Quarterback," *TheACC.com*, Sept. 26, 2007, http://www.theacc.com/sports/m-footbl/spec-rel/092607aaa.html?DB_OEM_ID=4200, July 14, 2010.

76 In 1966, Duke coach Tom Harp . . . someone to throw to.": Sumner, "Looking Back: Duke's Leo Hart."

76 "entered a football world . . . cloud-of-dust football.": "Leo Hart - (2008)," *www.ncshof.org*, http://www.ncshof.org/inductees_detail.php?i_recid=279, July 16, 2010.

76 Harp had noticed that . . . who went 53 yards for a touchdown.: Sumner, "Looking Back: Duke's Leo Hart."

76 We never thought it would . . . touchdown I ever had.: Sumner, "Looking Back: Duke's Leo Hart."

77 "the most sought-after high school player in the country": Shane Battier, "Knocking at Victory's Door," *Duke Magazine*, May-June 1997, http://www.dukemagazine.duke.edu/alumni/dm16/shane.html, July 22, 2010.

77 "I knew we had . . . That was my role.": Featherston, p. 107.

77 "established himself as . . . shooters in college basketball.": Featherston, p. 107.

77 "I was a good shooter . . . for that to pay off,": Featherston, p. 107.

77 [Chip Engelland} helped me . . . to change my shot.:

Featherston, p. 107.

78   they seemed like an unlikely . . . All three delivered.": Luke De-
Cock, "Finding Greatness," *The News & Observer,* April 6, 2010,
p. 3CC, http://nl.newsbank.com/sn-search/we/Archives?p_
action=dopc&p_docid=12F0E9020D1D8, July 22, 2010.

78   Duke "attacked, controlled, . . . a turning point for us," DeCock.

78   "arguably the most . . . weeks of the tournament.": DeCock.

78   "is a dream come true. It just is.": Ken Tysiac, "No Holding Back
Duke," *The News & Observer,* March 29, 2010, p. 1C, http://
nl.newsbank.com/nl-search/we/Archives?p_action-doc&p_
docid=12F0E8F8B2D1, July 22, 2010.

79   As sophomore reserve Hayes . . . anything to do with it.": Sumner,
Tales from the Duke Blue Devils Hardwood, p. 30.

79   Bradley changed his practices . . . to the full-court press.: Sumner,
Tales from the Duke Blue Devils Hardwood, p. 31.

79   With 14 minutes left, . . . the ball to Bucky Allen: Sumner, *Tales from
the Duke Blue Devils Hardwood,* p. 31.

79   It was almost like . . . He must have been psychic.: Sumner, *Tales
from the Duke Blue Devils Hardwood,* p. 31.

80   Duke guard Abby Waner came up . . . from the right corner: Rachel
Carter, "One Possession Dandy for Devils," *The News & Observer,* Dec. 8, 2006.

81   "The only fouls that . . . blocking, [or] charging,": Brill, p. 31.

81   the goals were true . . . pushed out by a broom.: Brill, pp. 31-32.

81   Play resumed with a . . . with all of our points: Brill, p. 32.

81   One of the Trinity . . . Wake Forest, Trinity's opponent.: Brill, p. 31.

81   An overflow crowd packed . . . that first-ever game: Brill, p. 32.

82   On a November night . . . displaying unbridled emotions.": Wahl.

82   There are three things . . think hard and talk.: Wahl.

83   hit with a technical foul . . . of the one-and-one.: Sumner, *Tales from
the Duke Blue Devils Hardwood,* p. 138.

83   "looked over to the bench . . . no one around but me.": Sumner,
Tales from the Duke Blue Devils Hardwood, p. 139.

83   On paper, it didn't make . . . and went with his instinct.: Sumner,
Tales from the Duke Blue Devils Hardwood, p. 139.

84   "knee-buckling touchdown pass . . . a firm handle on [the] game.":
Luciana Chavez, "Duke Defeats Vanderbilt," *The News &
Observer,* Oct. 26, 2008.

84   "We did a lot of things . . . not going to be denied.'": Chavez.

84   "We're always going to go out there thinking it's on us,": Chavez.

84   Duke played very well . . . everything we tried to do.: Chavez.

85 "a classic point guard . . . the ball and playing defense.": Sumner, *Tales from the Duke Blue Devils Hardwood*, p. 129.

85 When he was a freshman, . . . in examining college life.": Sumner, *Tales from the Duke Blue Devils Hardwood*, p. 129.

85 Nessley constantly had to . . . pizza under the covers.: Sumner, *Tales from the Duke Blue Devils Hardwood*, p. 130.

86 "How in the world . . . leave off Steve Acendark?": Sumner, *Tales from the Duke Blue Devils Hardwood*, p. 63.

86 the respective locker rooms . . . He didn't have to tell me twice.": Sumner, *Tales from the Duke Blue Devils Hardwood*, pp. 31-32.

86 only seven Blue Devil players . . . joined Verga in the lineup.: Sumner, *Tales from the Duke Blue Devils Hardwood*, p. 71.

87 You're out for the whole . . . . what he wanted to hear.": Brill, p. 136.

87 In the summer of 1994, . . . but he kept on working.: Brill, p. 135.

87 he could hardly walk, . . . to get back to his job.": Brill, p. 136.

87 He had to take a whole . . . refused even to consider it.: Brill, p. 136.

87 This is your job whenever you're ready to come back.: Brill, p. 136.

88 "I just hit the ball.": Edward G. Robinson III, "Golf Is Her Passion, Not Her Chore," *The News & Observer*, May 3, 2009.

88 Blumenherst always wanted . . . I just hit the ball.": Robinson.

88 I think God made . . . accept Him and believe.: Bettinger, p. 47.

89 Brand left with Mike Krzyzewski's blessing,: Brill, p. 142.

89 "I could understand . . . was hanging over him.": Brill, p. 153.

89 "It hurt my feelings . . . [Maggette and Avery] would leave.": Brill, p. 153.

89 Realistically, I'm not shocked . . . like this will happen.: Brill, p. 153.

90 For much of the season, . . . Duke were being padded.: Brill, p. 43.

90 the most famous arenas in the country at the time.: Brill, p. 43.

90 The official scorekeepers had . . . statistics rightfully indicated.: Brill, p. 44.

91 a "historic upset" that was deemed "pivotal" to the program.: Laura Keeley, "Duke 13, No. 16 Virginia Tech 10," *News Observer.com*, Oct. 27, 2013, http://nl.newsbank.com/nl-search/we/Archives?p_action-doc&p_docid=149BA251CD970CB8.

91 Not just for sixty . . . it all counts.": Kelly, "Duke 13, No. 16 Virginia Tech 10."

91 Ross Martin became the . . . in the same game.: "Duke Picks Off Logan Thomas 4 Times," *ESPN.com*, Oct. 26, 2013, scores.espn.go.com/ncf/recap?gameid=332990259.

91 You're going to have to be mentally tough the entire time.": Keeley, "Duke 13, No. 16 Virginia Tech 10."

BIBLIOGRAPHY

Anderson, Kelli. "Devil's Due." *Sports Illustrated*. 25 Nov. 2002. http://sportsillustrated.cnn.com/vault/article/magazine/MAG1027611/index.htm.

Battier, Shane. "Knocking at Victory's Door: A Basketball Diary." *Duke Magazine*. May-June 1997. http://www.dukemagazine.duke.edu/alumni/dm16/shane.html.

Bettinger, Jim & Julie S. *The Book of Bowden*. Nashville, TN: TowleHouse Publishing, 2001.

Brill, Bill. *Duke Basketball: 100 Seasons: A Legacy of Achievement*. Champaign, IL: Sports Publishing L.L.C., 2004.

Bill Brill and Mike Krzyzewski. *A Season Is a Lifetime: The Inside Story of the Duke Blue Devils and Their Championship Seasons*. New York City: Simon & Schuster, 1993.

Carr. A.J. "Duke Erupts for 34 First-Quarter Points." *The News & Observer*. 14 Nov. 1999. 1CC.

---. "Duke QB Ready for Long-Awaited Start." *The News & Observer*. 24 Sept. 1999. 6C.

---. "Duke Savors 28 Straight." *The News & Observer*. 23 Jan. 2000. 1C.

---. "Mr. Tough Guy: Leatherneck Attitude Comes Naturally to James." *The News & Observer*." 29 Jan. 2000. 1C.

---. "Pierce Overcomes Family Tragedy." *The News & Observer*. 2 Sept. 1999. 6C.

---. "Twice the Work, Twice the Payoff: Duke Senior Bailey Offers Insight into the Grueling Practice Schedule." *The News & Observer*. 21 Aug. 2007.

Carter, Rachel. "One Possession Dandy for Devils: Eight-Point Sequence Seals Victory over Commodores." *The News & Observer*. 8 Dec. 2006.

Chansky, Art. *Blue Blood: Duke-Carolina: Inside the Most Storied Rivalry in College Hoops*. New York City: Thomas Dunne Books, 2006.

Chavez, Luciana. "Duke Defeats Vanderbilt." *The News & Observer*. 26 Oct. 2008.

Dahlberg, Bruce T. "Anger." *The Interpreter's Dictionary of the Bible*. Nashville: Abingdon Press, 1962. Vol. 1. 135-37.

DeCock, Luke. "Finding Greatness." *The News & Observer*. 6 April 2010. 3CC.

Deford, Frank. "A Lost Weekend in Carolina." *Sports Illustrated*. 20 Dec. 1965. http://sportsillustrated.cnn.com/vault/article/magazine/MAG1078028/index.htm.

Doyel, Gregg. *Coach K: Building the Duke Dynasty*. Lenexa, KS: Addax Publishing Group, Inc., 1999.

"Duke Football Timeline." *Pursuit of Excellence: 2009 Duke Football*. 166-71. http://www.goduke.com/ViewArticle.dbml.

"Duke Picks Off Logan Thomas 4 Times, Upsets No. 14 Virginia Tech." *ESPN.com*. 26 Oct. 2013. scores.espn.go.com/ncf/recap?gameid=332990259.

"Duke Rush End Patrick Bailey Has Signed a Free-Agent Contract with the NFL's Pittsburgh Steelers." *The Devil's Den*. 29 April 2008. http://duke.scout.com/2/751036.html.

Eisenberg, Jeff. "Christian Laettner's Mom Cried When He Chose Duke over UNC." *rivals.com*. 30 June 2008. http://rivals.yahoo.com/ncaa/basketball/blog/the_dagger/post/Christian-Laettner-s-mom.

Featherston, Alwyn. *Game of My Life: Duke: Memorable Stories of Blue Devils Basketball*. Champaign, IL: Sports Publishing L.L.C., 2007.

Ferreri, Eric. "Life Is Sweeter at the Top for Duke Blue Devils." *The News & Observer*. 7 April 2010.

Gardner, Michelle. "No Mama's Boy." *South Florida Sun Sentinel*. 23 Oct. 1996. http://articles.sun-sentinel.com/1996-10-23/news/9610220681_1.

Harris, Tom. "Blue Devils Come Alive in Death Valley." *The News & Observer*. 19 Oct. 1980. 1-II.

Keeley, Laura. "Duke 13, No. 16 Virginia Tech 10: New Day, New Duke." *NewsObserver.com*. 27 Oct. 2013. http://nl.newsbank.com/nl-search/we/Archives?p_action=doc&p_docid=149A251CD970CB8.

-----. "Duke Ready for 'Greatest Challenge.'" *The News & Observer*. 25 Nov. 2013. http://nl.newsbank.com/nl-search/we/Archives?p_action=doc&p_docid=14A55A7636A4B948.

Krzyzewski, Mike with Donald T. Phillips. *Five-Point Play: Duke's Journey to the 2001 National Championship*. New York City: Warner Books, Inc., 2001.

Lazarus, Danielle. "DeVon Edwards Plays Unlikely Hero for Duke Football." *The Chronicle*. 11 Nov. 2013. http://www.dukechronicle.com/articles/2013/11/11/devon-edwards-plays-unlikely-hero-duke-football.

"Leo Hart - (2008)." *ncshof.org*. http://www.ncshof.org/inductees_detail.php?i_recid=279.

MacArthur, John. *Twelve Ordinary Men*. Nashville: W Publishing Group, 2002.

"Nate James Bio." *GoDuke.com*. 6 May 2008. http://www.goduke.com/View/Article.dbml?DB_OEM_ID=

4200&ATCLID=1458688.

"National Champions! Duke Defeats Cal to Capture First National Title." *GoDuke.com*. 20 May 2009. http://www.goduke.com/View Article.dbml?DB_OEM_ID=4200&ATCLID=3740746.

"No. 24 Duke Beats North Carolina 27-25." *Sports Illustrated*. 30 Nov. 2013. http://sportsillustrated.cnn.com/football/ncaa/gameflash/2013/11/30/53985/index.html.

"Patrick Bailey '08." *Office of News & Communications: Duke University*. 27 Nov. 2006. http://www.dukenews.duke.edu/2006/11/bailey.html.

Pickeral, Robbi. "Devils Drive Away Doubters." *The News & Observer*. 6 April 2010. 5C. http://nl.newsbank.com/nl-search/we/Archives?p_action=doc&p_docid=12F0E902D097A, July 22, 2010.

---. "Duke Plays Familiar Role Again: the Villain." *The News & Observer*. 3 April 2010.

Robinson, Edward G. III. "Duke Women's Import Has Polish." *The News & Observer*. 24 Dec. 2009.

---. "Duke's Lewis Leaves His Mark." *The News & Observer*. 27 Nov. 2009.

---. "Golf Is Her Passion, Not Her Chore." *The News & Observer*. 3 May 2009.

---. "Harding Returns to Duke to Have Jersey Retired." *The News & Observer*. 20 Jan. 2008.

Stevens, Patrick. "Costabile Supplies Clincher for Devils." *The News & Observer*. 1 June 2010.

Sumner, Jim. "1954 [sic] Orange Bowl: Duke 34, Nebraska 7." *GoDuke.com*. 2 Oct. 2004. http://www.goduke.com/ViewArticle.dbml?&DB_OEM_ID=4200.

---. "Looking Back: A Look Inside Duke's Gridiron Success in the Early 1960's." *TheACC.com*. 26 Sept. 2006. http://www.theacc.com/genrel/092606aaf.html.

---. "Looking Back: A Triple Overtime Classic in the Duke-Carolina Rivalry." *TheACC.com*. 21 Feb. 2008. http://www.theacc.com/sports/m-baskbl/spec-rel/022108aac.html.

---. "Looking Back: Duke Track & Field Sensation Dave Sime." *TheACC.com*. 16 April 2008. http://www.theacc.com/sports/c-track/spec-rel/041608aaa.html.

---. "Looking Back: Duke's 13-Year Run in Women's Tennis." *TheACC.com*. 5 May 2009. http://www.theacc.com/sports/w-tennis/spec-rel/050509aaa.html.

---. "Looking Back: Duke's Leo Hart Revolutionized the ACC at Quarterback." *TheACC.com*. 26 Sept. 2007. http://www.theacc.

com/sports/m-footbl/spec-rel/092607aaa.html?DB_OEM_ID=4200.

---. "Looking Back: Patience Paid Off for Duke's Anthony Dilweg." *The ACC.com*. 17 Sept. 2008. http://www.theacc.com/sports/m-footbl/spec-rel/091708aad.html.

---. "Sixty-Minute Man." *GoDuke.com*. 26 July 2004. http://www.goduke.com/ViewArticle.dbml?&DB_OEM_ID=4200.

---. *Tales from the Duke Blue Devils Hardwood*. Champaign, IL: Sports Publishing L.L.C., 2005.

Tiede, Joe. "Duke's Road to 1961 Bowl Was a Cotton-Picking Grind." *The News & Observer*. 6 Dec. 1989. 1C.

---. "Emotions and Points Flow as Duke Completes Mission." *The News & Observer*. 19 Nov. 1989. 8B.

---. "One in a Million -- 21-7." *The News & Observer*. 1 Oct. 1989. 1B.

---. "TD Pass on First Play Calmed Brown's Nerves." *The News & Observer*. 5 Nov. 1989. 14B.

Tudor, Caulton. "Blue Devils Make Statement." *The News & Observer*. 1 June 2010.

---. "Stunned Tigers Say Blue Devils Simply Played 'a Lot Tougher.'" *The News & Observer*. 1 Oct. 1989. 9B.

Tysiac, Ken. "Devils Draw Inspiration." *The News & Observer*. 5 April 2010. 1C. http://nl.newsbank.com/nl-search/we/Archives?p_action=doc&p_docid=12F0E9005BE5A.

---. "No Holding Back Duke." *The News & Observer*. 29 March 2010. 1C. http://nl.newsbank.com/nl-search/we/Archives>p_action=doc&p_docid=12F0E8F8B2D1D.

Wahl, Grant. "The Duke Way." *Sports Illustrated*. 21 Nov. 2005. http://sportsillustrated.cnn.com/vault/article/magazine/MAG1113830/index.htm.

"Wallace Wade Stadium." *Duke University Libraries: University Archives*. http://library.duke.edu/uarchives/history/histnotes/wade_stadium.html.

"Wallace Wade Stadium." *Pursuit of Excellence: 2009 Duke Football*. 42-43. http://www.goduke.com/ViewArticle.dbml.

Weiss, Dick. *True Blue: A Tribute to Mike Krzyzewski's Career at Duke*. Champaign, IL: Sports Publishing L.L.C., 2005.

NAME INDEX
(LAST NAME, DEVOTION DAY NUMBER)

SCRIPTURES INDEX
(by DEVOTION DAY NUMBER)

BLUE DEVILS